East Coast Main Line Locomotive Haulage

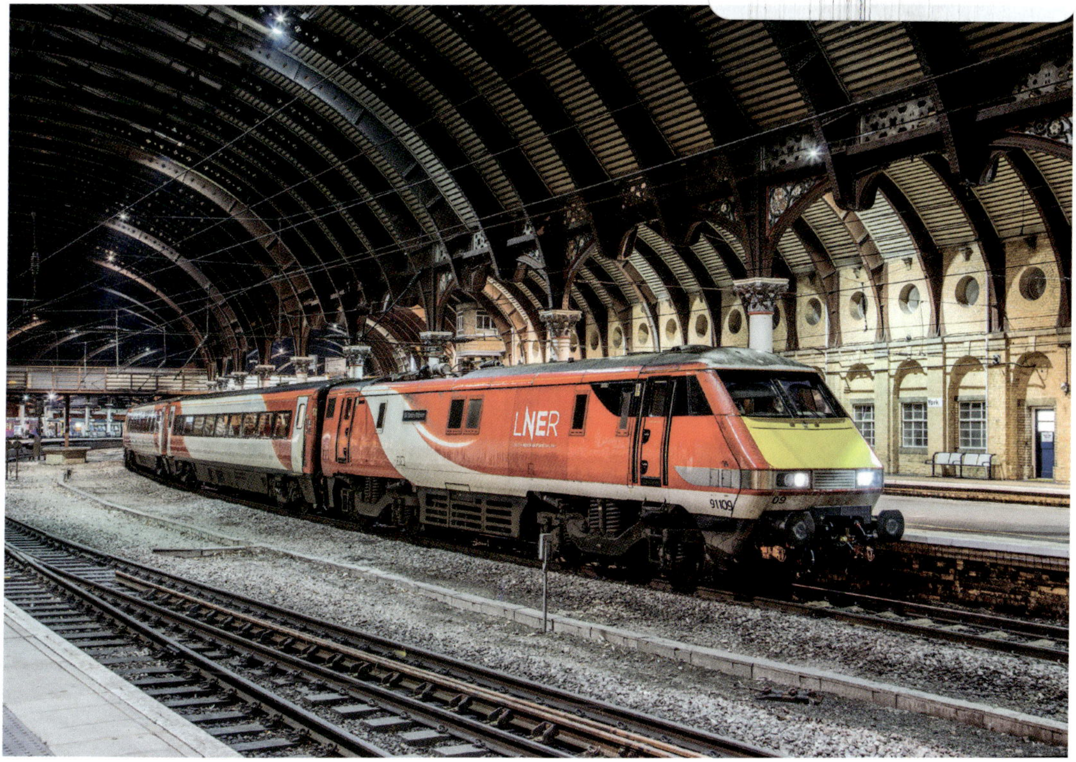

ANDY FLOWERS

KEY Books

BRITAIN'S RAILWAYS SERIES, VOLUME 37

Front cover image: On 10 January 2022, 91109 waits at Leeds, ready to propel the 16.45 departure south to King's Cross.

Back cover image: On Saturday 19 September 1998, a Deltic returned to a service train on the East Coast Main Line (ECML) after D9000, usually allocated to a Virgin CrossCountry Birmingham to Ramsgate and return diagram, was sent to Newcastle on the 1E33 10.00 Paignton–Newcastle. The loco returned south to Birmingham on the 1V67 17.53 Newcastle to Bristol Temple Meads.

Title page image: On 14 November 2019, 91109 waits to leave York on a King's Cross to Edinburgh service.

Contents page image: On 17 October 2019, 91125 waits at Edinburgh Waverley before taking empty stock out to Craigentinny depot.

Published by Key Books
An imprint of Key Publishing Ltd
PO Box 100
Stamford
Lincs PE19 1XQ

www.keypublishing.com

The right of Andy Flowers to be identified as the author of this book has been asserted in accordance with the Copyright, Designs and Patents Act 1988 Sections 77 and 78.

Copyright © Andy Flowers, 2022

ISBN 978 1 80282 349 3

All rights reserved. Reproduction in whole or in part in any form whatsoever or by any means is strictly prohibited without the prior permission of the Publisher.

Typeset by SJmagic DESIGN SERVICES, India.

Contents

Chapter 1	Introduction	4
Chapter 2	Route Description	8
Chapter 3	Steam Locomotives	12
Chapter 4	Pre-grouping Locos to BR Standards	28
Chapter 5	Local Services	30
Chapter 6	Branch Trains	33
Chapter 7	Steam on Passenger	34
Chapter 8	The Flying Scotsman	36
Chapter 9	The End of Steam	39
Chapter 10	Dieselisation	42
Chapter 11	Main Line Diesel Locomotives	44
Chapter 12	King's Cross Suburban Diesels	53
Chapter 13	Prototypes and Occasional Passenger Locos	56
Chapter 14	High Speed Trains	71
Chapter 15	Shunters	75
Chapter 16	Electric Locomotives	76
Chapter 17	Azumas	87
Chapter 18	Nationalisation to Privatisation	89
Chapter 19	Performance	94
Chapter 20	The Future	95

Chapter 1
Introduction

The withdrawal of the Class 91s from service on the East Coast Main Line (ECML) over the next few years will end an almost 180-year-long history of prestigious, high-speed express locomotive-hauled trains on the route, perhaps the most famous high-speed main line in the country, with a wealth of famous locomotives and trains having graced its tracks.

The 393-mile-long line linking London King's Cross with Edinburgh via York was largely built in the 1840s by three separate companies: the Great Northern Railway (GNR), the North Eastern Railway (NER) and the North British Railway (NBR), but before the advent of the GNR, it was termed initially the 'London and York'.

Completion of the line was as follows:

GNR: King's Cross to Shaftholme Junction (just north of Doncaster), completed in 1850.
NER: Shaftholme Junction to Berwick-upon-Tweed, completed in 1871. Before this, through trains ran via Knottingley.
NBR: Berwick-upon-Tweed to Edinburgh, completed in 1846.

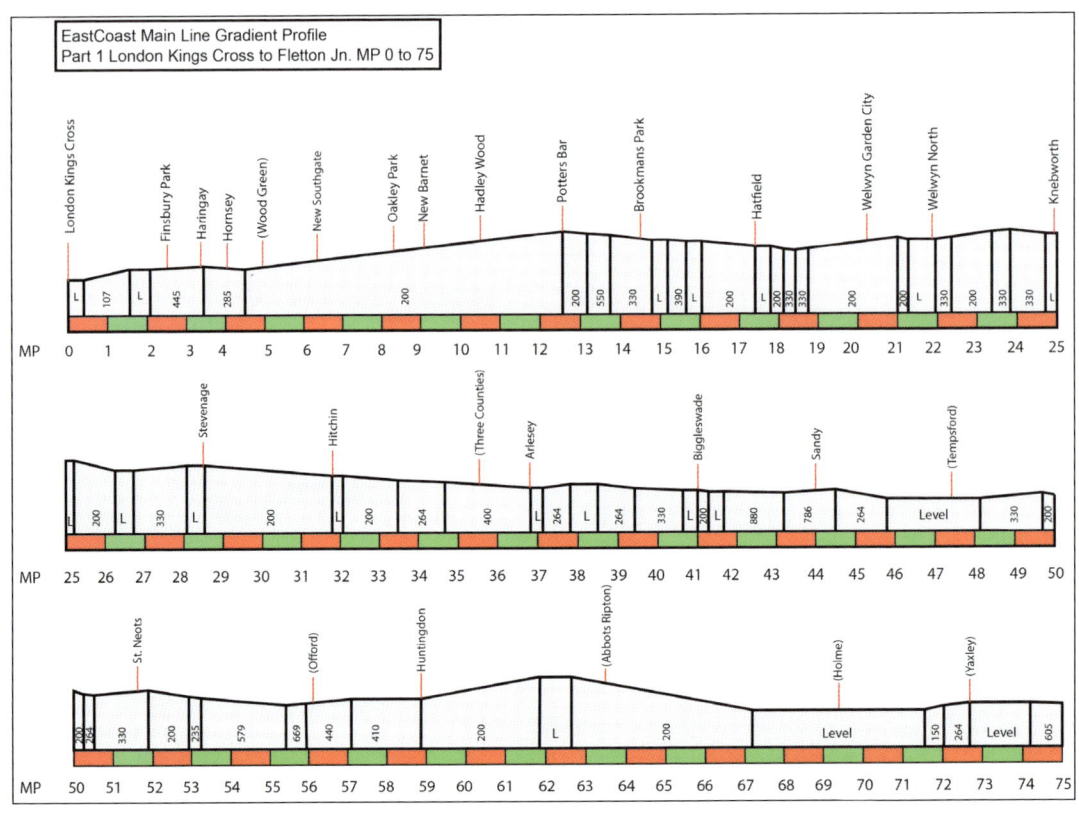

Introduction

In 1923, the three owners of the line were 'grouped' to form part of the London North Eastern Railway (LNER) and, from this point on, the new company competed with the London, Midland and Scottish Railway's (LMS) West Coast route for Anglo-Scottish traffic.

The ECML today is mostly four-track throughout between London and Stoke Tunnel, just south of Grantham, apart from the notorious bottleneck through Welwyn North and between Fletton Junction (near Peterborough) and Holme Junction. From Grantham northwards, the line is double track except for four-track sections near Retford, Doncaster and between Colton Junction and Darlington. From there northwards, the line is mostly double track to Edinburgh.

Gradients over the core ECML are relatively easy compared to the West Coast Main Line (WCML) route, with, surprisingly, one of the biggest challenges coming straight out of King's Cross, with a gradient of up to 1 in 107 facing departing expresses. Even the legendary Stoke Bank is no steeper than 1 in 178 near the summit and varies between 1 in 200 and 1 in 300 for much of its length. Perhaps the sternest test on the ECML, though tame by comparison to the hills of the WCML, is the four miles at 1 in 96 faced by up services climbing from Cockburnspath to the summit near Grantshouse, between Dunbar and Berwick-upon-Tweed.

The alignment of the main line has been altered at a few locations since originally opened, including:

- King Edward VII Bridge – opened in Newcastle in 1906.
- The Selby Diversion between Temple Hirst (just south of Selby) and Colton Junction – opened in 1983.
- Penmanshiel – the collapse of the tunnel on 17 March 1979 saw the diversion of a number of trains via Carlisle. Poor rock conditions prevented the tunnel reopening, and a new alignment was built in a cutting just to the west. The line reopened on 20 August the same year.
- Dolphinstone – 2km of track was moved in 2002 to avoid a speed restriction due to ground conditions.

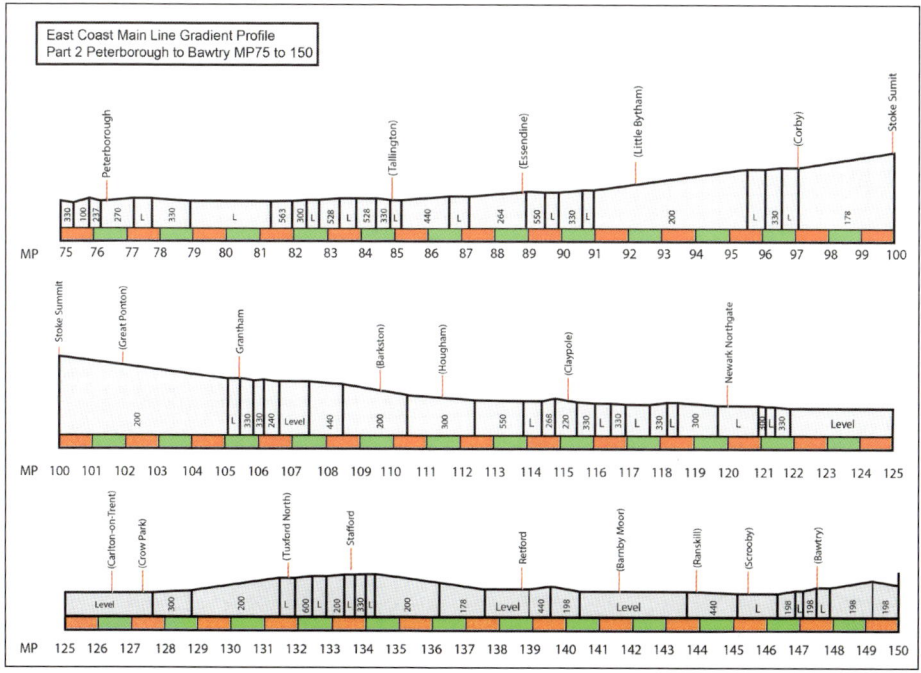

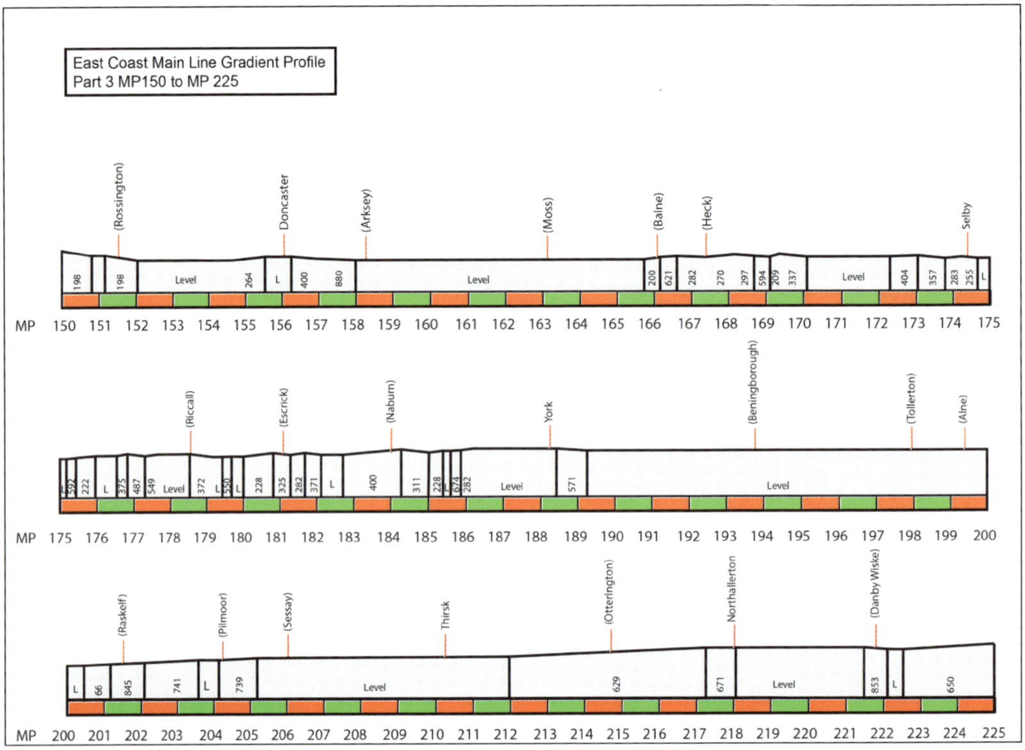
East Coast Main Line Gradient Profile
Part 3 MP150 to MP 225
(Rossington)
Doncaster
(Arksey)
(Moss)
(Balne)
(Heck)
Selby
(Riccall)
(Escrick)
(Naburn)
York
(Beningborough)
(Tollerton)
(Alne)
(Raskelf)
(Pilmoor)
(Sessay)
Thirsk
(Otterington)
Northallerton
(Danby Wiske)
MP 150 151 152 153 154 155 156 157 158 159 160 161 162 163 164 165 166 167 168 169 170 171 172 173 174 175
MP 175 176 177 178 179 180 181 182 183 184 185 186 187 188 189 190 191 192 193 194 195 196 197 198 199 200
MP 200 201 202 203 204 205 206 207 208 209 210 211 212 213 214 215 216 217 218 219 220 221 222 223 224 225

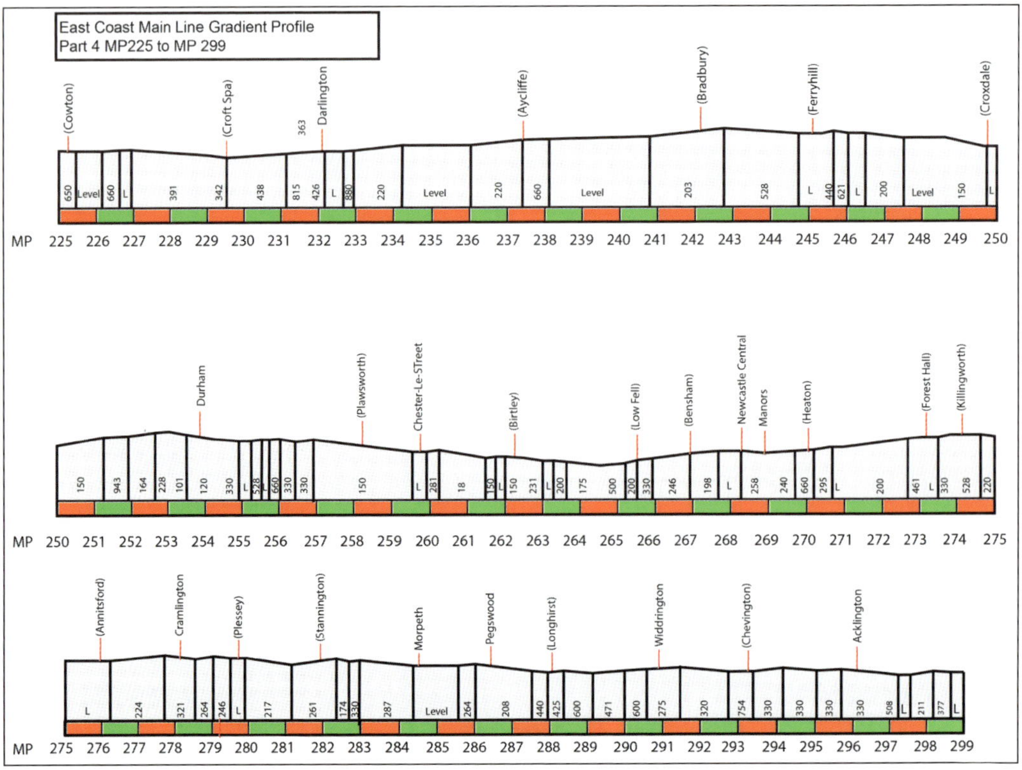
East Coast Main Line Gradient Profile
Part 4 MP225 to MP 299
(Cowton)
(Croft Spa)
Darlington
(Aycliffe)
(Bradbury)
(Ferryhill)
(Croxdale)
Durham
(Plawsworth)
Chester-Le-STreet
(Birtley)
(Low Fell)
(Bensham)
Newcastle Central
Manors
(Heaton)
(Forest Hall)
(Killingworth)
(Annitsford)
Cramlington
(Plessey)
(Stannington)
Morpeth
Pegswood
(Longhirst)
Widdrington
(Chevington)
Acklington
MP 225 226 227 228 229 230 231 232 233 234 235 236 237 238 239 240 241 242 243 244 245 246 247 248 249 250
MP 250 251 252 253 254 255 256 257 258 259 260 261 262 263 264 265 266 267 268 269 270 271 272 273 274 275
MP 275 276 277 278 279 280 281 282 283 284 285 286 287 288 289 290 291 292 293 294 295 296 297 298 299

East Coast Main Line Gradient Profile
Part 5 MP 299 to Drem
(Warkworth)
Alnmouth
(Longhoughton)
(Little Mill)
(Christon Bank)
(Falloden)
Chathill
(Newham)
(Lucker)
(Belford)
(Smeafield)
L 980 L 220 264 L 170 264 203 L 150 225 L 573 381 Level 559 Level 420 Level 200 L 208 L 264 300 L
299 300 301 302 303 304 305 306 307 308 309 310 311 312 313 314 315 316 317 318 319 320 321 322 323 324 325
(Beal)
(Coswick)
(Scremerston)
(Tweedmouth)
Berwick
(Burnmouth))
(Ayton)
(Peston)
Level 377 Level 230 190 L 245 490 L 200 L 190 400 L 400 L 500 250 200 600 200
MP 325 326 327 328 329 330 331 332 333 334 335 336 337 338 339 340 341 342 343 344 345 346 347 348 349 350
(Grantshouse)
(Cockburnspath)
(Innerwick)
Dunbar
East Linton
(East Fortune)
Drem
200 500 L 200 96 210 L 750 Level 200 300 L 360 L 600 L 300 L 250 L 400 L 400 L 300
MP 350 351 352 353 354 355 356 357 358 359 360 361 362 363 364 365 366 367 368 369 370 371 372 373 374 375

East Coast Main Line Gradient Profile
Part 6 Drem to Edinburgh Waverley
Drem
Longniddry
Prestonpans
(Inveresk)
(New Hailes)
(Joppa)
(Portobello)
Edinburgh Waverley
300 L 300 L 300 L 300 L 500 L 500 L 300 L 300 L 300 L 300 L 400 L 300 L 78 L
375 376 377 378 379 380 381 382 383 384 385 386 387 388 389 390 391 392 393

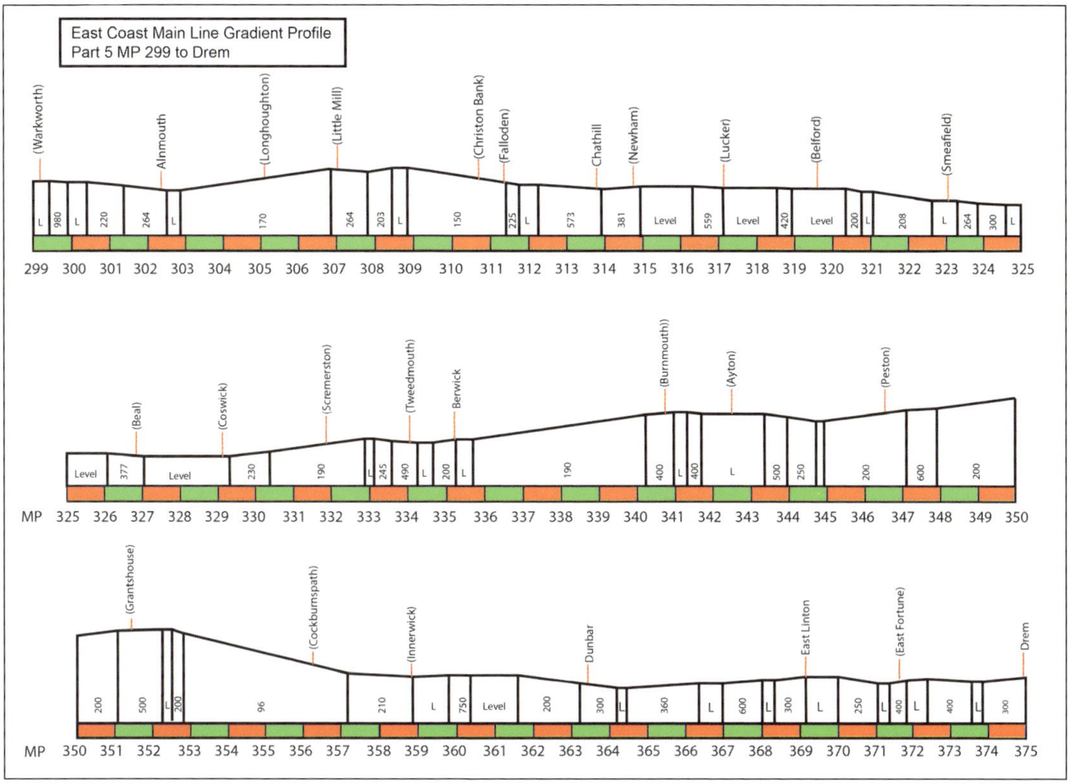

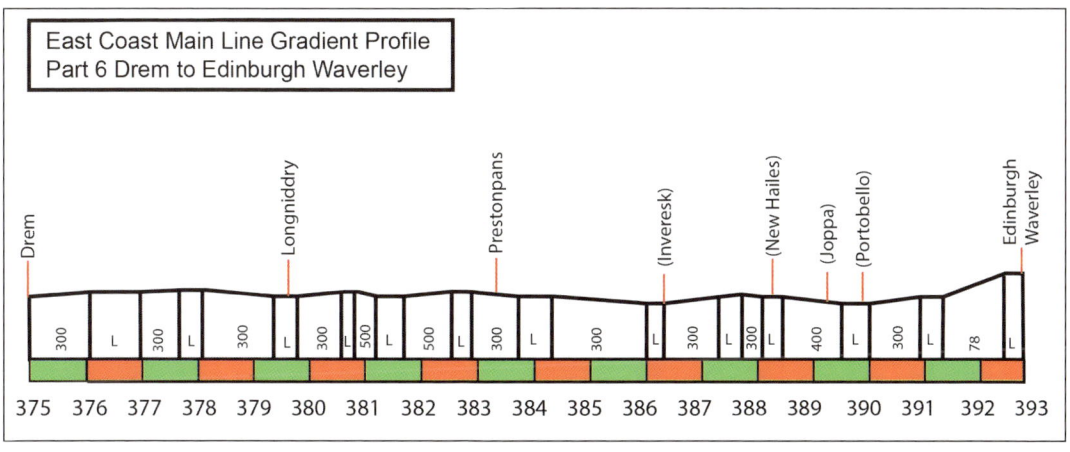

Chapter 2
Route Description

King's Cross station was opened in 1852, which was relatively late compared to other London termini, with just one arrival and one departure platform with 14 sidings. Tracks were covered with an impressive 71ft-span twin-arched roof designed by Lewis Cubitt, but compared to the adjoining designs of St Pancras and Euston, the new station was much more functional.

Expanding levels of suburban traffic meant that by 1875 a new station was needed, which was built alongside the original in order to accommodate extra platforms. With traffic growth continuing, more platforms were added in 1892–93, replacing some covered sidings.

The King's Cross area is thought to be the site of the last battle between Queen Boudica and the Romans, and legend has it that she is buried beneath Platform 8.

With North London at the time not being as densely populated as the area to the south, the ECML was not built with suburban traffic in mind, the core purpose being a fast route to the north. The Hertford Loop, while today a major suburban railway, was originally of importance as a diversionary route for freight off the main line and also for fast passenger services rerouted during engineering work or emergency closures.

Development of housing north of London saw the line expand to four tracks for the first 100 miles, with a six-track section between Finsbury Park and Wood Green. The exception was the 2½-mile-long double track bottleneck from Welwyn Garden City over Digswell Viaduct and on to Woolmer Green Summit.

Major housing development in the 20th century saw new 'garden cities' created in Welwyn and Letchworth and an expansion of Stevenage. Urban development has mostly stopped north of Hitchin, and the line passes through a 40-mile stretch of flat agricultural land. Peterborough was a source of delays for many years, owing to speed-restricted curves with a limit of 20mph through the station. In 1972, BR remodelled the station area, providing high speed through lines.

The East Coast loop line (part of the Great Northern and Great Eastern Joint Railway and more commonly known as the 'Joint Line') ran from Whitemoor to Spalding and took much of the freight traffic between the busy yards of Doncaster and Whitemoor away from the ECML.

The 'Joint Line' was later used for the testing of experimental locos on freight including HS4000 *Kestrel* in 1969 and 47601, the testbed for the Ruston 16RK3CT power unit that went on to be fitted in the Class 56s. The line was also used as an engineering diversion route off the ECML and brought a range of relief trains to the Spalding Flower Show with unusual locomotive types, including Southern Region Class 33s and Hastings DEMUs. Also, occasionally, Class 50s travelled to or from Doncaster Works for overhaul via the 'Joint Line'.

Today, the line still hosts diversions off the main East Coast route and also operates a light passenger service, provided by East Midlands Railway utilising DMUs. Additionally, LNER now operates a King's Cross to Lincoln service with five trains a day using Azuma units. Four out of the five services take the 'Joint Line'.

From Peterborough, the ECML heads north over a ridge of hills including the famous 1 in 178 Stoke Bank then down at 1 in 200 from Stoke Summit through the market town of Grantham and on to Newark and Retford.

Even though the ECML had been constructed by a number of separate small companies, particularly north of York (before amalgamation under the NER), the intention was to form a main Anglo-Scottish

Route Description

Above: **55008** *The Green Howards* leaves York on 14 September 1981 on the 08.07 to King's Cross. (Andy Flowers Collection)

Left: D362 (later 40162) arrives at York in August 1966 on 1S56, the 08.45 Leeds to Aberdeen service, hauling a mixed rake of Mk.1 and Mk.2 stock. (Andy Flowers Collection)

route, and, accordingly, the line has been aligned largely straight and level between major conurbations along the overall route. North of York, the line crosses the agricultural Plain of York, largely straight and level to Darlington, this 44-mile and ten chains section has long been known as the 'racing stretch'.

From Darlington, the surrounding scenery becomes hillier, the line crossing wooded river valleys and a number of viaducts approaching Durham, with an impressive viaduct carrying the railway above the town, with the famous cathedral on its horseshoe bend visible to the right on the east/up side. The ECML levels out again towards Newcastle, passing Tyne Yard and with the Angel of the North on the hillside on the east side before reaching Newcastle.

The line finally reaches sight of the east coast at Alnmouth, passing the long beaches facing Lindisfarne, with the foothills of the Cheviots to the west. The line then crosses the famous

Above: An unidentified Class 91 crosses the Royal Border Bridge into Berwick on a late evening King's Cross to Edinburgh service on 18 September 1991. (Andy Flowers Collection)

Right: 91101 *Flying Scotsman* stands at King's Cross on 8 June 2021 with 1A31, the 13.15 to Leeds. The loco has been re-vinyled into a 'Flying Scotsman' livery by current operator London North Eastern Railway (LNER).

Royal Border Bridge before entering Berwick station, built through the medieval castle in an act of architectural and historical vandalism.

Climbing northwards, steep inlets offer spectacular views of the North Sea before heading inland again through the hill country of Lammermuir and up to the summit at Penmanshiel, the tunnel here having been abandoned after its collapse in March 1979, closing the line for five months. Heading down Cockburnspath Bank brings the line back to the coast of East Lothian. At Drem Junction, just east of the eponymous station, the branch from North Berwick joins on the right.

After passing a succession of southeast Edinburgh commuting stations and Craigentinny depot on the down side, the line approaches the impressive station of Edinburgh Waverley, with the volcanic features of Arthur's Seat and the Salisbury Crags looming over the city to the south west.

Chapter 3
Steam Locomotives

A huge array of steam and diesel locos have worked over the ECML, particularly on stopping services over short stretches of the route. No article can hope to cover all the different types of locomotives that have appeared, though hopefully the following will give a flavour of the variety seen and reported over the years. Much has been written of the exploits of the main classes, such as Deltics, Pacifics and HSTs, but here I will be focusing on some of the lesser-known players in the history of motive power over the ECML.

Since the first train left King's Cross on 14 October 1852 (the 07.00 to York, hauled by a Great Northern Crampton single), the route has seen a vast range of different motive power types. These range from the original locos built for the constituent companies of the GNR, NER and NBR, on to the LNER Pacifics, then the British Railways Standard steam types, through the first main line diesels, then Deltics, HSTs, and, following electrification, the Class 91s, and right up to today's introduction of the Azuma EMUs.

The various British steam locomotive classes have by convention been named on the basis of the locomotive superintendent of the owning company. For example, in the case of the GNR, and later

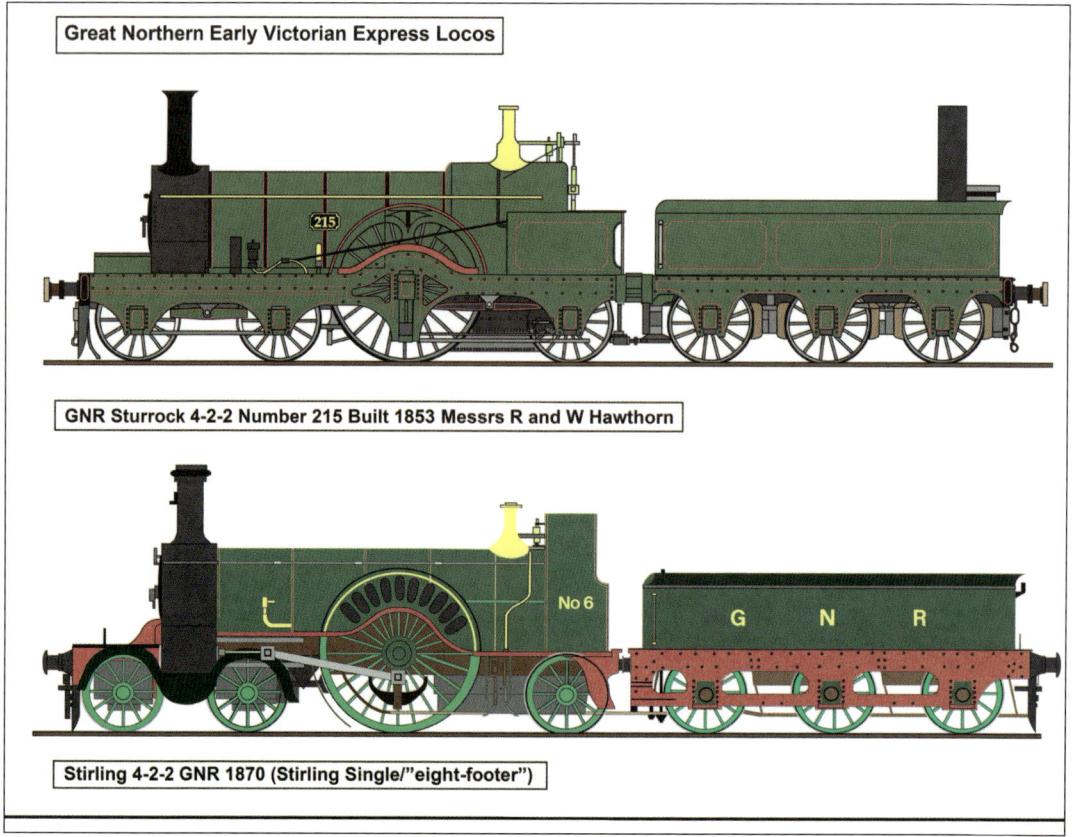

Great Northern Early Victorian Express Locos

GNR Sturrock 4-2-2 Number 215 Built 1853 Messrs R and W Hawthorn

Stirling 4-2-2 GNR 1870 (Stirling Single/"eight-footer")

LNER, the locomotives used on the express services out of King's Cross were named after Sturrock, Ivatt and then Gresley. The first passenger locomotives of the GNR were:

  1–50 'Little Sharpies': 18.5t 2-2-2s from Sharp Roberts and Co.
  51–70 'Small Hawthorns': 27t 2-2-2s from R&W Hawthorn.

Along with the goods types of the time, most proved ineffective and were rebuilt as tank engines for branch line duties.

Archibald Sturrock was appointed as locomotive superintendent of the GNR in 1850, overseeing the opening of the GNR main line and the design and ordering of a wide range of modern steam locomotives. These featured higher boiler pressures, 150lb per square inch as opposed to the traditional 100lb, with enlarged fireboxes and grates to increase steaming rates.

Apart from the 4-2-2 experimental express loco 215 of 1853 and a number of 7ft 2-2-2 singles and 2-4-0 express types, Sturrock also produced a range of tank engines for GNR suburban duties, including F5 0-4-2Ts. Sturrock also converted a number of 'Little Sharps' into passenger tank locos in 1852–53.

The GNR's main workshops were moved from Boston in 1852 to a new facility in Doncaster, despite much lobbying for it to be built in Peterborough. Doncaster Works became widely known as 'The Plant' and became famous for loco construction, though it was initially opened as a maintenance and repair centre before locos began to be built there from 1867.

The first steam locos working out of King's Cross, the GNR Cramptons, were soon rebuilt by Sturrock as conventional singles, together with 50 other new build 0-6-0 types. From 1875, Stirling 8ft singles began to be allocated to 'Top Shed' (the large steam shed just north of the terminus) for GNR express work with a number of Stirling four-coupled designs generally used on secondary express duties.

Original GNR Postcards, clockwise from top left: express passenger engine No.1 (Stirling single, 1870); eight-wheeled coupled goods No.401 (1901); express No.272 (1904); and six-wheeled coupled goods (1911). (GNR)

When Ivatt took over as chief engineer in 1896, he continued with the singles tradition, building 11 new examples in 1900–01 and a number of 4-4-0s. However, in a revolutionary break from tradition, he introduced the first Atlantic (4-4-2) loco in the UK, No. 990, built in 1898. The type went on to become known as 'Klondykes'. The first large-boiler C1 Atlantics began to be built from 1902 onwards, with the 8ft Stirling singles withdrawn from main line work by 1907 as the new locos took over most top-link work.

Up until 1913, Stirling 7ft 6in singles and Ivatt 4-4-0s still made appearances on some lighter express workings. By 1914, the singles lost their top-link work, although the Ivatts lasted for several decades longer.

With NER locos responsible for haulage of through trains to Edinburgh, this company, together with the GNR, shared responsibility for express services on the ECML up to the grouping. Initially, this saw the GNR using 2-2-2s and 4-2-2 singles as far as York and the NER taking trains forward using, initially, single driver 2-2-2 locos (including the famous 'Jenny Lind' and the 450 Class) with 2-4-0s for freight work. By the 1870s, the NER favoured the 2-4-0 wheel arrangement for express passenger locos rather than the single wheel drivers with 0-6-0s for freight. Edward Fletcher's '901' Class 2-4-0s were often used on the top-link Edinburgh duties between 1860 and 1890.

When Alexander McDonnell took over as the NER's chief engineer in 1883, he began to standardise the wide array of locomotives used, favouring a 4-4-0 arrangement for passenger locomotives, including his famous '38' Class, which turned out to be less capable than the previous 901s. After McDonnell retired in 1884, having been in the post for less than two years, a committee headed by Henry Tennant introduced 20 2-4-0s for passenger work before Thomas William Wordsell was

GNR Class C1 990 (LNER C2) is seen near London with fellow GNR Atlantic 251 on the down run of the Doncaster Works Centenary 'Plant Centenarian' tour on 20 September 1953. Both locos were brought out of retirement for the special. (Andy Flowers Collection)

Class C1 Great Northern Railway Ivatt large boiler Atlantic 4-4-2 express passenger steam locomotive 4430 approaches New Barnet in a scene from the 1930s with a semi-fast service, the train formed of mostly LNER stock. (Andy Flowers Collection)

appointed in 1885 and he introduced a successful series of 4-4-0s. He was succeeded by his brother, Wilson Wordsell, who developed the 4-4-0 designs, including the M and Qs and finally the highly successful R Class, which remained in service right up until 1957. Wordsell also introduced the V Class 4-4-2s (Atlantics) in 1903, although these proved less effective than the Rs.

Sir Vincent Raven took over in 1910, introducing the Class Z Atlantic, another successful design which lasted in service until 1948. Raven introduced the first Pacifics on the NER, shortly after World War Two, for use on the line north of Newcastle, although, upon the grouping, the LNER favoured an alternative design produced by his successor, Sir Nigel Gresley, for the GNR.

Anglo-Scottish services needed engine changes at Grantham, York and Newcastle. Later services were entrusted to 4-4-0s before the appearance of Gresley's modified 'Large Atlantics' and the NER's Raven 4-6-0s. Just prior to the grouping, the GNR introduced Gresley's first Pacifics, 1470 and 1471. Larger boilers and a pressure increase from 180psi to 220psi led to a reclassification from A1 to A3, the first loco uprated being 1480N/4480 *Enterprise*, outshopped in July 1927.

The LNER went on to build more Pacifics than any other railway, a type well-suited to the continuous high-speed running of the ECML. By the start of World War Two, the 100-strong fleet of Gresley A1, A3 and A4 Pacifics powered most of the ECML express services with the Class C1 Ivatt Large Atlantics still appearing (mainly south of York) together with the Raven Class C7 Atlantics and Gresley Class D49s (mainly north of York). Around the same time, the Gresley V2s were beginning to appear, partly ousting the older types.

Nigel Gresley designed a powerful 'Mikado' (2-8-2) to haul East Coast services over the more steeply graded line onwards from Edinburgh to Aberdeen, a line where double-heading of the conventional Pacifics used on the core ECML was not allowed. The new locos were designated as Class P2s. The locos, built between 1934 and 1936 at Doncaster Works, were all given emotive Scottish names, including the famous *Cock of The North* and *Wolf of Badenoch*. All six members of the class were eventually streamlined in a fashion similar to the A4s.

Thompson decided to convert the six locos into Pacifics (as A2/2s) and built four further A2/1s at Darlington Works in 1944, with 15 A2/3s produced under Thompson and another 15 Peppercorn A2s built at Doncaster. Further building was halted following nationalisation in 1948, the A2s having gained a reputation for high coal use and heavy maintenance requirements, although they were powerful and dependable. One member of the class was preserved, this being 60532 *Blue Peter*.

In the case of the NBR, the classification of locomotives was more complex, not aided by the number of locomotive superintendents in charge; the first five being sacked or resigning following scandals or incompetence. Additionally, the designation letters for locos were often duplicated. The NBR adopted its own unique locomotive designs, from the original 2-2-2s built at Hawthorns, through the Cowlairs-built Wheatley 2-4-0s, the more familiar Drummond, then Holmes, 4-4-0s up to the final Reid 4-4-2s and 4-4-0s.

On the NBR, Reid introduced the North British Atlantics of Classes I and H for top-link trains, later classified as LNER Classes C10 and C11. These were replaced by A1 Pacifics by the LNER, although they occasionally worked specials up to the late 1920s.

With the NER, many older locomotive types were inherited on its formation from the amalgamation of a number of smaller companies. The first chief superintendent to begin to standardise its locomotive fleet and introduce new designs on a large scale was Thomas William Wordsell. The Wordsell brothers' successor, Vincent Raven, took over as the last of the NER's chief mechanical engineers in 1910 and introduced larger designs for the ECML, including the S3 4-6-0s (reclassified as B16s by the LNER) and the Pacific 4-6-2s, later A2s under the LNER. The LNER continued to build many of Raven's designs following the grouping in 1923.

Ivatt D2 (LNER D4) 4-4-0 4370 stands at Gainsborough Lea Road on 27 May 1933 on a 'Joint Line' stopping service. This loco amply demonstrates the complexity of the renumbering carried out on some LNER locos, as they passed through pre-grouping to the LNER then finally to British Railways; in this case, it was variously numbered 1370, 4370, 2173 (2nd LNER number) and finally British Railways 62173. (Andy Flowers Collection)

Ivatt C1 Atlantic 4-4-2 4445 nears Potters Bar on an up semi-fast service in the early 1930s. (Andy Flowers Collection)

Edward Fletcher of the NER designed the 901 Class 2-4-0s, with 55 built between 1872 and 1882. They were used on the fastest York to Newcastle and Newcastle to Edinburgh expresses. The NER later specialised in large-wheeled 4-4-0s for its express locomotives, generally working Anglo-Scottish expresses between York and Edinburgh.

The Class M1 4-4-0s were Wilson Wordsell's first express passenger locomotives design, built between 1892 and 1894. He went on to build large numbers of Class M and Class Q/Q1 4-4-0 locomotives for use on East Coast express passenger services, these were all later classified as D17s by the LNER. The M and Q classes were at first displaced by D20s (NER Class R) on express services before Wordsell's C6 (Class V) and Ravens C7 (NER Class Z) Atlantics displaced the 4-4-0 locos on top link duties.

The Class Q locos generally displaced the Class M1s from the very best of the top jobs, but both could still be found working alongside each other on the main line. Three years later, the new D20s displaced both the Class Q and Class M1 engines from many of their main line duties. Between 1910 and 1918, the even larger C6 and C7 Atlantics were introduced, displacing all of the NER's 4-4-0s to secondary duties.

Raven introduced the Z Class 4-4-2s (C7 under the LNER) in 1911, these being Britain's first three-cylindered express passenger types. Wilson Wordsell also introduced the V Class 4-4-2s from 1903, reclassified as C6 by the LNER. After the grouping, the C6s and C7s began to stray away from the northeast, occasionally reaching King's Cross, before being displaced by Pacifics and V2s in the 1930s.

Wordsell's NER Class S 4-6-0s (LNER Class B13) were designed for East Coast express duties north of York, with 40 built between 1899 and 1909. They proved to be poor steamers and were soon replaced by the Class R 4-4-0s. The NER Class S1 4-6-0s (LNER Class B14) were also designed by Wilson Worsdell with five locomotives built between 1900 and 1901 at Gateshead Works. The S1 had

2743 *Felstead* passes Greenwood, north of New Barnet, on a southbound express in the late 1930s, with the train formed largely of Gresley-designed teak stock. A number of experiments and modifications were made to the Gresley A1 Pacifics in the late 1920s, and 2743 became the first of the new Class A3 Super Pacifics, the rebuilding of which was completed in August 1928 with an uprated 220psi boiler. (Andy Flowers Collection)

larger driving wheels than the S Class with a higher boiler pressure. The fleet was also used on heavy passenger services between York, Newcastle and Edinburgh with more success, although they were gradually replaced on these services by NER Class R and NER Class R1 4-4-0s. After 1907, they had been largely relegated to hauling fish trains.

Twenty of the NER Raven-designed S2s (LNER B15) 4-6-0s were built between 1911 and 1913 and after initially featuring on some express traffic, they were replaced by the three-cylinder Class Z (LNER C7) Atlantics. They were relegated to mixed traffic duties, for which they were originally designed. They then became regular performers on excursions over the northern end of the ECML, being noted on trains to Scarborough.

Gresley introduced a 2-6-0 design in 1912–13, the H3 'Ragtimers' (later K2s), and they appeared regularly on relief passenger duties on the East Coast. These were followed in 1920 by the H4s, later to be termed K3s by the LNER, which went on to be built in larger numbers. From summer 1923, a number of ex-Great Central (GC) locos started to appear on the East Coast, including B3 4-6-0s (famously used on the Harrogate Pullman) and C1s, although the GC locos proved largely unsuccessful on these duties. Further north, Atlantics were still much in evidence, including Worsdell C6s, Raven C7s and C8 compounds.

The first GNR 1470 Pacifics were introduced in 1922, and Gresley carried on with his design for the LNER, designating it as A1. Improvements to the design of the A1s saw the introduction of the A3 'Super Pacifics' in the late 1920s, with another 27 examples built from new and conversions carrying on until as late as 1949. The A1 Pacifics represented a step up in terms of performance over the earlier Atlantics. On test, 1471 hauled a 20-coach (200t) train from London to Grantham, averaging 51.8 mph. From 1928, they were working the non-stop 'Flying Scotsman'.

Under Gresley, the LNER introduced a large-scale programme of locomotive replacement, with the iconic Pacific designs, A2, A3 and A4, to the fore for high-speed passenger work together with the V2 'Green Arrow' 2-6-2s and the 'B' 2-6-0s for secondary work.

Class V2 60850 on a down fast goods service approaching Brookmans Park in 1953. The V2s were a true mixed traffic type and were equally at home on heavy fast goods services like this as they were substituting for Pacifics on express passenger workings. (Andy Flowers Collection)

The Gresley W1 10000 'Hush-Hush' was an experimental locomotive built by the LNER and the only 4-6-4 tender steam loco built in Britain. (Andy Flowers Collection)

Upon the formation of the LNER, most of the expresses out of King's Cross continued to be hauled by Ivatt Atlantics, plus the two Doncaster-based Gresley Pacifics, with piloting of heavier trains (over 450t) by 4-4-0s or Gresley N2s as far as Potters Bar, with the 4-4-0s occasionally working through to Peterborough.

The semi-fasts had a wider range of locos, including Ivatt 4-4-0s of classes D1, D2 and D3 and Gresley K2 2-6-0s. On the GN stopping services, ex-NLR 4-4-0Ts were still widely used, gradually

Thompson A2/3 4-6-2 60516 *Hycilla* passes through the now closed station of Holgate, just south of York, its home shed, on an up semi-fast service in 1956. (Andy Flowers Collection)

being replaced by LMS Standard 3F 0-6-0T 'Jinties' and Gresley N2 0-6-2Ts, together with a few Hill GER Class L77 (LNER N7s) and the Ivatt N1 0-6-2Ts. The A1 Pacifics gradually took over the majority of top-link services from the older steam types in the 1920s.

The iconic streamlined Gresley A4 Class, introduced in 1935, achieved the highest verified numbers of more than 100mph running of any British steam locos and proved to be not only good performers but also reliable and efficient. On 27 August 1936, 2512 *Silver Fox* reached 113mph down Stoke Bank, a record for the highest speed recorded with steam on a UK service train.

During and after World War Two, Edward Thompson was responsible for the successful B1 4-6-0s and, post-nationalisation, the LNER's last chief engineer, Arthur H. Peppercorn, introduced the popular A1 Pacifics. While none of the A1s survived into preservation, the new-build loco 60163 *Tornado* continues to fly the flag for East Coast steam power with every prospect of another long-lost type, Gresley's P2 2-8-2s (the 'Cock of the North' class) also being resurrected in the next few years.

The complicated classification system inherited by the LNER was simplified by the addition of lettering suffixes as follows:

- B: ex-NBR
- C: ex-GCR
- D: ex-NER
- E: ex-GER
- N: ex-GNR
- S: ex-GNS

In 1924, a further change was announced with the decision to renumber all pre-grouping locos, except NER ones, which kept their original numbers.

Gresley A3 60110 *Robert The Devil* on an up express at Doncaster in the mid-1950s. (Andy Flowers Collection)

By 1939, most of the pre-grouping classes had been relegated from top-link duties or withdrawn, with Gresley Pacifics of classes A1, A3 and A4 in charge, supported by Gresley D49 4-4-0s and Raven Class C7 4-4-2s on some secondary and piloting duties on the northern section, and Ivatt Class C1 Atlantics performing similar duties on the southern half of the line.

During World War Two, services out of King's Cross were cut by around 50 per cent and timings extended, with an average speed of only 45mph. The remaining trains were often loaded up to 25 coaches (almost 800 tons), although loadings were more generally 16–20. This was still a severe challenge for the Pacifics, with banking assistance needed out of the terminus and locos often way off the platforms and into the tunnel area.

Rare wartime workings included the appearance of Austerity 2-8-0 7084 on the 10.15 Leeds–King's Cross, replacing a failed loco. B2 5425 also made an appearance on the 17.55 King's Cross to Peterborough on 11 April 1944. B1s began working Cambridge expresses from 1944 and were also noted later on semi-fast services such as the 'Butlins Express' to Skegness. B1s were also used between Newcastle and York on Liverpool 'Trans-Pennine' services.

The end of the war saw a large-scale withdrawal of the Ivatt Atlantics, with the type relegated to menial work by 1947, largely replaced by B1s. Also following the end of the war, Great Eastern locos, including B12s, started to make an appearance on the line.

Unusual loco appearances on passenger services continued after 1945. On 1 July 1946, J39 0-6-0 2951 appeared at King's Cross on the 17.13 from Cambridge, and, on the same day, the 17.50 from Hitchin featured Ivatt D3 4309. Another interloper on the 17.13 from Cambridge two days later was D9 4-4-0 6040. Ex-GE J19/2 0-6-0 4654 appeared on the 17.10 King's Cross–Royston on 3 September 1946, with cousin J20 8279 seen at King's Cross in September of the same year. On 11 October 1948, streamlined B17 61659 appeared at the London terminus on a train from Cambridge.

A4 Pacific 60028 *Walter K Wigham* **passes through Hornsey on 12 June 1961 on the down 'Elizabethan', the 09.30 King's Cross–Edinburgh. The loco was in very clean condition, having hauled the Royal train from King's Cross to York four days earlier for the Duke of Kent's wedding. (Andy Flowers Collection)**

The LNER announced plans in mid-1947 to build 25 100mph-capable 1600hp diesel-electrics for East Coast expresses, designed to work in pairs and replace 32 Pacifics, despite 84 Pacifics being on order at the time. With this plan dropped, steam retained its exclusive hold on the line for another ten years.

By 1948, at the time of the formation of British Railways, East Coast expresses were mainly in the hands of Gresley and Thompson Pacifics aided by Gresley V2s. There was no large-scale reclassification of the inherited loco classes, although renumbering of the locomotives was carried out on the basis of former owning companies.

Peppercorn A1 Pacifics began to be introduced on Hull and Leeds trains, and despite the nationalisation of the railways, and the introduction of newer Pacifics like the Peppercorn A1s and A2s together with the new 'Standard' steam designs, the tried and tested Gresley Pacifics retained their hold over the ECML's top-link express duties right up until the introduction of diesels in the 1960s. The Britannia Pacifics made only a few appearances on the East Coast, including Immingham-based examples on King's Cross to Cleethorpes services.

The 1948 Locomotive Exchange Trials saw a variety of Grouping locos appear on test on the East Coast including ex-GWR 4079 *Pendennis Castle* and King 6018, LMS Royal Scot 46162, Coronation 46236 and ex-SR Merchant Navy Class 35019, replaced by 35017. All the 'foreign' locos were assessed against the indigenous A4s, particularly those now fitted with Kylchap double chimneys. All classes of loco performed well, keeping to time, but the A4s were generally agreed to have been the most impressive performers.

In the summer of 1949, the 17.25 Royston–Welwyn Garden City was worked by Cambridge locos, bringing a number of unusual types to the area including B17s, J15 E5391, J39 4820 and L1 67712. Claud Hamilton 4-4-0s were also noted together with C12 67354. Other rare visitors included GC Atlantic 2903 on a nine-coach relief from Lincoln on 26 July 1947. Another rare working on 8 August 1953 was B16 61420 on the 14.30 King's Cross–Leeds as far as Grantham. B16s were also noted on some Hull services in the 1950s.

In the late 1950s, Gresley K3/2 2-6-0 61925 drifts through the centre road at Doncaster on an up goods service. The loco was withdrawn from its home depot (Doncaster itself) in 1961. (Andy Flowers Collection)

Class A1 60129 *Guy Mannering* on the ECML near Essendine (Stoke Bank) in the late 1950s. (Andy Flowers Collection)

The LNER maintained Gresley B17 4-6-0 61671 *Royal Sovereign* in immaculate condition and readily available for Royal train duties to Sandringham, although it could be found on some King's Cross–Cambridge timetabled services when not on royal duty.

In July 1952, King's Cross saw its first diesel shunter, Hornsey-allocated 12112, an LMS design later to be designated as Class 11. Following this initial success, from January 1956, diesel shunters 13158–61 were delivered to King's Cross. These locos, designated DEJ7, then D3/5, 3/1C and finally Class 10, successfully replaced many of the smaller steam shunters in the area.

From 1954, new steam types began to work the King's Cross suburban duties including Fowler 2-6-4Ts

In 1955, the unique W1 Class 4-6-4 60700 started work on Doncaster–King's Cross services. In the same year, a Black 5 and a BR Standard 5 appeared on King's Cross to Cambridge services in connection with AWS trials. Following on from this, in 1957, Standard 5s were allocated to King's Cross in exchange for V2s for use on Cambridge trains. Another steam type seen on King's Cross workings was Robinson's ex-GCR OO tanks (LNER A5) 4-6-2Ts, which were trialled in the late 1920s, and again when 69814 was transferred from Lincoln in 1958, mostly for empty stock workings. K1s also began to appear on some Cambridge trains after World War Two, with Britannias later on some Hull services and a few Standard 4 tanks used on commuter services from King's Cross.

The years 1961 to 1963 saw most of the ECML Pacifics withdrawn from traffic, and by the winter of 1964, steam had more or less finished in the northeast, with Haymarket ending all steam operations at the same time.

A1 Pacific 60146 *Peregrine* heads a northbound express at Essendine (north of Peterborough) in the summer of 1959. *Mallard* created the world speed record for steam just north of this point. (Andy Flowers Collection)

Class A3 60039 *Sandwich* **stands at York in a scene from the early 1960s, working a down East Coast express while an unidentified Class 40 stands in the centre road with 3G32, the 16.30 fast parcels service from York to Newcastle. (Andy Flowers Collection)**

Class A3 60039 *Sandwich* **on the ECML near Essendine (Stoke Bank) in the late 1950s. (Andy Flowers Collection)**

Above: **A4 4494** *Osprey* **passes Langley water troughs, near Stevenage, on a down fast express in the late 1930s. (Andy Flowers Collection)**

Left: **N2/4 69575 takes empty stock out of King's Cross in May 1959. (Andy Flowers Collection)**

Gresley N2 0-6-2T 69524 leaves King's Cross on a train for Hertford on 5 June 1954. B16 4-6-0 61640 *Somerleyton Hall* waits in the background. (Andy Flowers Collection)

Class V2 4841 is just north of Potters Bar on a down semi-fast service in the 1930s. The coaching stock includes a GN BCK and an elderly Great Northern clerestory coach. (Andy Flowers Collection)

Steam officially ended on the ECML in 1965 with a steam-hauled York–Newcastle and return relief on 31 December, this last official train being hauled by A1 60145 and was reported to have reached 102mph near Thirsk. The last 12 ex-LNER Pacifics were finally withdrawn in 1966.

Chapter 4
Pre-grouping Locos to BR Standards

Pre-grouping locos
A large number of pre-grouping steam types could be seen at points like York, Doncaster and Peterborough up until the 1930s.

Aspinall's Lancashire and Yorkshire Class 7 'Highflyer' Atlantics were regular sights at York from 1899, working trains for Manchester over the line southwards. Built in two batches of 20 at Horwich Works, all of the class survived into LMS days, the last being withdrawn by 1934.

Up to the start of World War One, a wide range of larger steam locos (4-4-0s and 4-4-2s) from a selection of companies were also outshedded at York. The railways comprised Great Northern, Great Eastern, Midland, Great Central and Lancashire and Yorkshire. Additionally, between 1893 and 1904, London and North Western Railway locos also appeared at York on cross Pennine services.

Pre-grouping railways that served the Doncaster area included the West Riding and Grimsby Railway, the Lancashire and Yorkshire, the South Yorkshire, the Great Northern/Great Eastern 'Joint Line', Dearne Valley and the Great Central. Similarly, pre-grouping railways that reached the Peterborough area included the Midland and Great Northern Joint, the Great Eastern, Midland and London and North Western Railways, with LMS types featuring in later years on cross-country traffic.

LMS locos
Midland Railway (MR) and then later LMS types could be seen at York, working cross-country services south over the ECML as far as Chaloners Whin, where the East Coast diverged left towards Selby and the cross-country traffic for Sheffield continued southwards.

'Flying Pig' Ivatt Class 4MT 2-6-0s were allocated to the Eastern and North Eastern regions in the early days of British Railways.

Southern locos
The allocation of ex-London, Brighton and South Coast Railway B4 4-4-0s 2051 and 2068 to York shed between 1941 and 1944, on loan from the Southern, made a strange sight on some secondary passenger services in the area. The LNER used them not only on some stopping services between Bridlington, York, and Leeds but also for piloting of Pacifics on heavily loaded ECML wartime expresses. Their efforts apparently wore the venerable locos out, and after they were returned to the Southern Railway in December 1944, they were withdrawn.

BR Standards
BR Standard types were never common performers over the ECML, the Eastern Region preferring its tried and tested Gresley Pacifics. Three BR Standard 5MTs (73157–59) were allocated to King's Cross in September 1957 and appeared on some semi-fast services, mostly to Cambridge or Peterborough, and a number of horse race specials to Newmarket.

A total of 13 Class 4 2-6-0s were allocated to the NER and were used on some local services in the northeast, including Durham to South Shields, together with the famous Newcastle to Blackpool trains via Stainmore. A number of Class 3 2-6-0 and 2-6-0Ts were based on the NER, with the Class 3 tanks working some trains out of Darlington on services to Penrith.

The Standard Class 2 2-6-0s famously worked out of Berwick on the line to St. Boswell via Kelso. Standard 4 2-6-4Ts were one of the more successful BR designs, and the small number allocated to York and Leeds sheds were reported on some local services.

Great Central Locos

On absorption into the LNER, a number of ex-GCR locos saw service on or around the ECML, including the Robinson 8F (B4 under the LNER) 4-6-0s, ten of which were allocated to Ardsley and Copley Hill in the 1920s. They were used mostly between Leeds and Doncaster and on the 'Yorkshire Pullman', appearing as far south as King's Cross. They continued to see use on the ECML after World War Two until replaced by the Thompson B1s by 1950.

Liveries

The various pre-grouping companies prior to the formation of the LNER had a range of different coloured steam locomotives, with many in black and grey (particularly Great Northern wartime austerity), but the colour green dominated. On the GNR, this was described as 'grass green' and on the North British, it was a much darker 'bronze green'. The North Eastern locos featured two types of 'Saxony green' with different shades for freight and passenger types.

With the dominance of green on its inherited loos, it became LNER policy to standardise on green for its locos, originally thought to be the 'grass green' of the GNR, although later referred to as 'apple green'.

Some special liveries were also applied, such as silver-grey for the first four A4 Pacifics used on the 'Silver Jubilee' services and later changed to 'garter blue' for A4s on the east coast's premier services. An experimental Royal blue livery was also applied to Thompson rebuilt Class A1 Pacific 4470 *Great Northern* in 1945. Lined black was applied as an austerity measure on some secondary passenger locos from 1928 onwards with freight locos reverting to plain black.

One other area of design that was introduced by the LNER was the use of the Gill Sans font, which was created by Eric Gill, an artist and rail enthusiast, in 1926. The use of Gill Sans was a tradition that carried on with British Railways, London Underground, Railtrack and even English, Welsh and Scottish Railways (EWS).

55019 *Royal Highland Fusilier* stands under the famous roof at York on 23 April 2005, with a railtour from King's Cross to Edinburgh.

Chapter 5
Local Services

A very wide range of tank engines were used on the many local services on the ECML and on the many branches that joined it; over 25 major junctions being present between King's Cross and Newcastle alone.

Fletcher's 0-4-4T bogie tank passenger, or BTP, (LNER G6) was introduced from 1874 on the NER to replace tender locos being used on branch lines.

Wordsell's 2-4-2T Class A (LNER F8) was introduced between 1886 and 1892 to replace the BTP type and they worked alongside G5 and G6s on northeastern branch lines and suburban services.

Stirling's 0-4-4Ts (LNER G1 and G2) were built between 1889 and 1895 and were used on London Great Northern suburban traffic.

Ivatt introduced his GNR C2 (LNER C12) Class 4-4-2Ts in 1898 for suburban traffic, initially in the West Riding of Yorkshire and later out of King's Cross. Some C12s lasted in service into BR times, working from King's Cross to Alexandra Palace, the last withdrawn as late as 1958.

One highly unusual trial in 1903 saw H1 Class 2-6-0s (imported at the turn of the century from American manufacturer Baldwin) used on King's Cross suburban traffic. The locos were reported to have performed better than the usual C2 4-4-2T tanks but needed to be turned and were very inefficient in terms of oil and coal usage.

Ivatt's N1 0-6-2T suburban tanks were introduced in 1907 as a replacement for his R1 0-8-2Ts and Stirling 0-4-4-Ts on Great Northern London suburban traffic. They were withdrawn, or moved on to light freight duties, from the mid-1920s.

Nigel Gresley's GNR N2 Class 0-6-2Ts were introduced in 1920, with further locos built under the LNER from 1925 onwards. They replaced the earlier C12 4-4-2Ts and N1s.

Hill's Great Eastern Railway N7 0-6-2Ts (LNER N70) were designed for the heavily loaded suburban services out of Liverpool Street and built between 1915 and 1924. They were highly successful and found use more widely under the LNER, including on Great Northern suburban stoppers out of King's Cross and Moorgate. They were also employed on suburban trains in the Glasgow and Edinburgh areas, the latter on services to North Berwick.

The Scottish N2s were replaced by V1s, and most of the Scottish fleet migrated to the London area, where some remained in service right until the end of steam in the area.

Edward Thompson's L1 2-6-4Ts were designed as a modern replacement for Gresley's N2 Class and were introduced in 1948 to Hitchin for use on outer-suburban duties. Hornsey acquired four L1s in December 1950 with King's Cross receiving six, mostly for empty stock duties. The new locos proved successful but never fully replaced the N2s, with both types still seen on Great Northern suburban duties right up until the end of steam.

Hill-designed GER Class C72 Class 0-6-0T 68654 (J68 under the LNER) was generally seen solely on shunting duties but made an appearance on the main line on 5 October 1957 on the Fridays-only armed forces leave Train from Henlow RAF Camp, running over the ex-MR Bedford Branch to King's Cross via Hitchin. The line from Bedford was built in 1858 to allow the MR access to King's Cross. Services were never frequent, and the line closed to passengers in 1961.

The Wordsell Class O (LNER G5) 0-4-4Ts provided haulage for many branch lines and local passenger services in the northeast from the 1890s to the 1930s, replacing a number of earlier

A4 Pacific 60032 *Gannet* **passes through Hornsey on 12 June 1961 on a King's Cross to Newcastle service. (Andy Flowers Collection)**

types and were replaced in turn on the heavier suburban traffic by newer tank locos of classes A8 and V1.

Ivatt's GNR D3 and D2 4-4-0s (later classified as D3 and D4 by the LNER) were introduced in the 1890s for secondary duties and worked many of the longer distance stopping services over the southern half of the ECML until the 1920s, together with some piloting duties, particularly with Stirling single-wheelers in their earlier years. In the early 1930s, six D3s were allocated to Darlington and worked local trains to Bishop Auckland, Saltburn and Barnard Castle.

In 1900, the D3s were concentrated over the south of the ECML, working secondary services and often piloting the larger Stirling single wheelers on heavier trains. By the start of World War One, the class were largely demoted to stopping services, duties they carried out until their eventual withdrawal.

Robinson's Great Central 9K and 9l classes (C13 and C14 under the LNER) of 4-4-2Ts could be seen on a number of trains passing near the ECML with C13s noted on Barnsley–Doncaster locals until the 1950s.

V1 2-6-2T s were introduced by Gresley in the 1930s, with some receiving higher pressure boilers and reclassified as V3s and a final batch built as V3s from new. Most of the fleet were based in Scotland, although some were tried on King's Cross to Hitchin trains in 1931. V3s also saw use on Newcastle–Middlesborough trains in the 1950s and also around Edinburgh.

Darlington shed received six D3s for stopping services in the area in the early 1930s. By the end of the war, the ex-GN Ivatt D3 4-4-0s had been very much demoted to minor duties. D2000 (ex-LNER 4075) was noted on a down local near Peascliff Tunnel, just north of Grantham, on 18 May 1948. The last D3 in service was 62000, this lasting until October 1951 with British Railways and was the last of the GNR 4-4-0s to remain in service.

In the northeast, the large A8 'Pacific Tanks' (4-6-2Ts) were Gresley rebuilds of Raven's LNER H1 Class 4-4-4Ts. They worked many suburban services, taking over from the G5 0-4-4Ts. The A8s were replaced in the 1950s by the introduction of DMUs.

London's N2 0-6-2Ts were often seen hauling high-capacity Quad-Art sets with four carriages mounted on five articulated bogies. Fowler Class 4 2-6-4Ts 42328 and 42374 were used on extended trials on Great Northern suburban services in the mid-1950s, although they never went on to replace the indigenous L1s and N2s.

Wordsell D20 and D21 4-4-0s were used on northeastern stopping services after being relegated from fast and semi-fast main line services. St. Margaret's-allocated Reid NBR Class K (LNER D34) 'Glen' 4-4-0s, built between 1913 and 1920, were noted on stopping services between Edinburgh and Berwick up until the late 1950s, together with V2s downgraded from their semi-fast express duties.

In a specially posed official shot in July 1937, five A4s built for 'The Coronation', a streamlined, high-speed service between London and Edinburgh, are displayed at Top Shed (King's Cross). On the right is 4482 *Golden Eagle* – the first of the class to be outshopped in the standard LNER ECML livery. (British Railways)

Chapter 6

Branch Trains

Over the years, a large number of interesting services and locomotives were used on the many branch lines that fed into the ECML.

The 'Ally Pally' push-pull workings between Finsbury Park and Alexandra Palace featured GNR Stirling G3 (658 Class) 0-4-4Ts, GNR C2 (LNER C12) 4-4-2Ts (from 1948 onwards) and ex-Great Central Pollitt F2 2-4-2Ts during World War Two and for a few years afterwards. N2s then worked most services until the branch closed in 1954.

Gresley's GNR K2 2-6-0s were often see at Grantham on stopping services to Nottingham.

The NER Class O (GNER G5s) were a widely used 0-4-4T type designed by William Wordsell. Built as early as 1894, some examples lasted in service almost to the end of steam (1958). They were widely used in the northeast and were also later used on push-pull services from Selby to Goole.

Robinson GCR Class Ns (LNER A5s) 4-6-2Ts featured on stopping trains in the northeast, particularly trains into Darlington from the Saltburn line, typically using Gresley non-corridor stock until the late 1950s. In the late 1920s, some were also used on King's Cross to Hitchin and Baldock stoppers. Durham never had a shed of its own, despite its size and importance and borrowed G5s for a number of duties including workings to Middleton-in-Teesdale.

More than just a branch line, the services from Newcastle Central to Hawick via Hexham are worthy of a mention, providing North Eastern enthusiasts with the sight of a variety of NBR types such as the Reid D30 'Superheated Scots' (NBR Class J) 4-4-0s built between 1914 and 1920.

Class D20 4-4-0s were used on the Alnmouth to Alnwick shuttles until the early 1960s, when K1 2-6-0s took over before DMUs were introduced in 1966, working the line to its closure on 29 January 1968.

Gresley V2 Class 60919 is near what is thought to be Nigg Bay, just south of Aberdeen, with the 15.30 West Coast Postal. The train included passenger coaches as far as Perth. (Andy Flowers Collection)

Chapter 7
Steam on Passenger

The high-speed nature of the ECML meant that freight locomotives were always rare on passenger duty, save for rescues and replacements for last-minute failures. Even in the case of rescues, freight locos were relatively uncommon, the powers that be having adopted a policy of ensuring suitable replacements or 'pilot locomotives' (usually Pacifics) were based at strategic locations along the route, and any failing loco usually limped along to a point where it could be replaced. Nevertheless, over the years a few notable freight locos appeared on passenger duty on the east coast.

In the late 1950s, 9Fs could be found working passenger services on the ECML in the summer months on King's Cross to Peterborough stoppers, though 92195 appeared on the 15.00 King's Cross to Newcastle on 15 August 1958, with 92184 on the 13.52 Leeds as far as Grantham the next day. This was timed at 90mph descending Stoke Bank on the return 'Heart of Midlothian', the highest speed ever recorded with the class and an amazing piece of locomotive performance from a small-wheeled 2-10-0 freight loco.

The Ivatt-designed J1s and J2s were designed as freight locomotives and were produced from 1908 as a tender version of the N1 tanks. Despite their freight designation, their good turn of speed saw them used on occasional passenger duties for much of their working lives. They could be seen on excursion traffic, with three of the locomotives noted on separate excursions to Skegness, all leaving King's Cross on the August Bank Holiday in 1909.

The Ivatt-designed J39 0-6-0s (with later locos produced under Gresley with minor modifications) were also ostensibly freight locomotives, though they could be seen occasionally on excursion traffic, particularly on King's Cross to Skegness summer specials. Before World War Two, some J39s were

Class V2 60966 passes through Haringey at speed on a down express from King's Cross in the late 1950s. (Andy Flowers Collection)

The amount of freight on the ECML has declined over the years and today is hard to path in the daytime, even on the slow lines. In easier times, WD/8 2-8-0 90331 trundles along the slow lines near Potters Bar in January 1960. (Andy Flowers Collection)

Gresley V3 2-6-2T 67635 arrives at Doncaster on an unknown date in 1959, hauling the Hull portion of the 'Yorkshire Pullman', which was usually a B1 duty. The Hull coaches were attached at Doncaster to a portion from Leeds, usually hauled by a V2 or A3, which took the combined train south to London. The powerful V3 was withdrawn in 1963. (Andy Flowers Collection)

noted on King's Cross-based suburban services with 3590 recorded on a pair of 'Quad Arts' on 13 May 1939. J39s were also used on the Alnmouth to Alnwick branch line.

Ex-Midland 4F 0-6-0s were also regular visitors through Peterborough in the 1950s and early 1960s, working stopping services between Peterborough East and Leicester. One rare loco appearance on a stopping service on the ECML itself took place south of Edinburgh with O7 Austerity 2-8-0 63182 (ex-WD 79185), noted on a local to the Scottish capital on 13 August 1948.

Chapter 8
The Flying Scotsman

The 'Special Scotch Express' through service began in 1862 and initially took ten hours to reach Edinburgh from London, including a half-hour lunch stop in York. By 1888, the journey time was down to eight and a half hours, but lunch had been cut to 15 minutes. The three operating companies on the route, GNR, NER and NBR, had formed the East Coast Joint Stock Group to provide coaches for the service, and the stock was used for through journeys until the grouping in 1923.

The first unofficial use of the name 'Flying Scotsman' was noted in *The Times* newspaper in 1875. The term became official in 1924 under the LNER, with the company advertising the trains under the new Scotsman branding, departing simultaneously at 10.00 from Edinburgh and London and giving flagship Pacific 4472 the same name. Since then, the line has become famous as the route of the Flying Scotsman, with many of the public confusing the name of the loco with the train itself.

4472 enhanced its growing reputation, and the legend of the name, on 30 November 1934, by becoming the first loco to officially reach 100mph near Little Bytham on a special test run from Leeds to London. In 1935, another LNER Pacific, A3 2750 *Papyrus*, reached 108mph at the same spot and

Class A1 4480 *Enterprise* **on a down express service just north of Potters Bar in 1939. The loco was later rebuilt as a Class A3. The train features a Gresley Corridor Twin brake composite 141-B GN 218CC, one of the first purpose-built articulated coaches in the UK. (Andy Flowers Collection)**

A4 Pacific 4482 *Golden Eagle* passes Langley Troughs, near Stevenage, with the down 'Flying Scotsman' on an unknown date in the late 1930s. (Andy Flowers Collection)

A4 Pacific 60003 *Andrew K McCosh* passes Everton, near Sandy, on an up express on 19 July 1952. (Andy Flowers Collection)

still holds the world record for highest speed by a non-streamlined steam loco, which is shared with a French Chapelon Pacific. As part of the 1930s atmosphere of competition with the LMS, the LNER's A4 4468 *Mallard* achieved a world record speed for steam of 126mph down Stoke Bank (on test) on 3 July 1938, a record that stands to this day.

The first diesel-hauled 'Flying Scotsman' featured Class 40 D201 on Saturday 21 June 1958, with regular diesel diagrams introduced shortly after with a '40' booked to work the down 'Talisman' (King's Cross–Edinburgh service) as far as Newcastle, it then returning south on the 'Aberdonian' (up sleeper service from Aberdeen).

From the summer of 1962, accelerated timings were introduced, taking advantage of the higher power of the new diesels. The 'Flying Scotsman' returned to a six-hour timing, the same as the steam-hauled 'Coronation' in 1937.

The last recorded steam haulage of the 'Flying Scotsman' took place on 9 December 1963, after A3 Pacific 60106 took over from a failed diesel at York, working forward to King's Cross.

From the new timetable in 1963, the Deltics were regularly reaching speeds of 100mph in service, with the Deltic-hauled 'Flying Scotsman' now achieving King's Cross to Edinburgh in five hours and 55 minutes. This included one stop at Newcastle and finally beat the pre-war six hours A4 Pacific schedule. By the mid-1970s, the overall time had been cut down by another half an hour, to five hours and 27 minutes.

LNER revived the 'Flying Scotsman' brand, a train which has been booked for Azuma units since 1 August 2019. The up 'Scotsman' is now timed for only four hours, leaving Edinburgh at 05.40.

'Flying Scotsman', the loco, has gone on to become world famous, even more famous than the titled train that gave it its name. Following withdrawal and preservation, 4472 has gone on to become part of the National Collection and travels nationwide on special workings. On 30 June 2001, the popular loco is ready to depart London Paddington for Plymouth on a special charter, shortly after its boiler pressure has been increased to 250lb/in. The author had been invited on board to time the train to help assess any performance improvements. The South Devon Banks, unfamiliar territory for a former East Coast racehorse, were conquered with ease.

Chapter 9
The End of Steam

While the first main line diesels (the English Electric Type 4s) were tested on the ECML as early as March 1958, their introduction was delayed, and reliability issues saw the Gresley Pacifics remain in top flight service into the mid-1960s. A3s that had been moved to the Great Central also returned to the GNR lines.

From the late 1950s onwards, a large number of farewell railtours were operated with some sparkling performances. 60007 *Sir Nigel Gresley* notably reached 112mph down Stoke Bank on the Stephenson Locomotive Society-organised 'Golden Jubilee Special' on 23 May 1959, which was a post-war steam speed record.

60013 *Dominion of New Zealand* heads an up express for London south of Newark in August 1962. (Andy Flowers Collection)

Class A1 4474 *Victor Wild* on a down express service, thought to be the 16.00 King's Cross to Leeds, just north of Potters Bar in the late 1930s. The loco was later rebuilt as a Class A3. (Andy Flowers Collection)

A4 Pacific 60021 *Wild Swan* storms through Potters Bar on a semi-fast express in the early 1960s. (Andy Flowers Collection)

On 21 September 1968, 4472 *Flying Scotsman* storms up Stoke Bank with the Locomotive Club of Great Britain 'The East Riding Limited' railtour. After 1968, steam was banned from Britain's main line network, with 4472 getting a derogation and a double tender to avoid water stops. (Andy Flowers Collection)

British Railways recognised that the reliable A3 and A4 Pacifics that were being replaced on the core ECML expresses by diesels still had a few more years of life in them. A number of A3s were moved to Leeds for Settle and Carlisle duties with A4s used on Glasgow to Aberdeen services.

The last true steam-hauled ECML service could be claimed to be the 14.20 Bradford Exchange to Leeds on 1 October 1967, the train conveying through carriages for King's Cross and ironically hauled by ex-LMS Black Five 45428, now preserved on the North Yorkshire Moors Railway.

The last part of the ECML to see regular steam in service was York, where London Midland locos, generally Black 5s, made sporadic appearances on services from the Manchester area, right up until 1967. On 29 December 1967, 70013 *Oliver Cromwell* worked the Fridays-only 17.47 Manchester Exchange to York, a duty allocated to a Kingmoor (12A) loco. With the shed closing on 1 January 1968, this is thought to have been the last timetabled steam service over the ECML.

Chapter 10
Dieselisation

The introduction of the first of the LMS 'twins' on the West Coast in 1947 appeared to spur the LNER into looking at its own modernisation plan to replace its steam fleet. A report that year, initiated by C. P. Hopkins and M. R. Bonavia, the assistants to the general manager (Peppercorn), concluded that the company's traffic difficulties were because of non-availability of steam locos, which in turn were due to shortages of coal, poor quality coal or the inability of workshops to deliver new locos. The use of diesels was proposed as the best option to overcome all of these issues.

The initial plan was for a fleet of 25 1,600hp diesels to work in pairs, the new locos being expected to have increased availability, better acceleration and higher performance on adverse gradients, together with better cleanliness and good publicity. The total cost of using two diesels per train compared to one Pacific was also favourable – 11.25p per mile compared to 12.7p.

Fourteen different quotes were obtained for the building of the fleet from various manufacturers, although the project was dropped on the advent of nationalisation. Ironically, this extended the life of steam on the ECML, as the new Eastern Region initially preferred to wait for electrification but delayed it in other areas of BR (particularly the Southern Region) by around ten years. Prior to the report, Edward Thompson brought in a five-year plan in 1945 calling for 1,000 new steam locos, mainly from private contractors.

D206 (later 40006) heads a northbound express at Essendine, north of Peterborough and on Stoke Bank, in the summer of 1959. (Andy Flowers Collection)

40025 stands on the 'blocks' at King's Cross on the 07.15 commuter service from Peterborough in late 1978. In another platform, a Class 31 has arrived with empty stock. (Andy Flowers Collection)

By 1963, the end for steam on British Railways was planned to be completed by 1972, but, by 1965, this was brought forward to the end of 1967, with a plan for steam to be replaced two regions at a time in 1965, 1966 and then 1967. The Eastern Region was planned to be one of the first regions to lose all its steam locos, together with the Western, as both were complaining of issues with fuel and staffing,

English Electric Type 4 D201 was used on the down 'Flying Scotsman' as far as Newcastle on 21 June 1958, heralding the start of the diesel era. The operating authorities noted that the new diesels did not offer the opportunity to greatly accelerate the steam schedules at the time and with reliability issues with the new types, steam remained in use on top-link duties into the early 1960s.

The diesels were initially expected to be a stopgap modernisation, as electrification from King's Cross and Moorgate through to Hertford and Letchworth was expected to be extended afterwards to Leeds and York. In the event, the higher traffic levels on the WCML provided a better case for the first main overhead electrification scheme in the 1960s, as BR and private industry were unable to provide enough physical resources to complete both schemes at the same time.

Chapter 11

Main Line Diesel Locomotives

The first of British Railways' production main line diesel locos to be delivered were the Brush Type 2s in November 1957, followed by the English Electric Type 4s in March 1958. The first English Electric Type 4 diesels were designated for Great Eastern duties, but their successful introduction saw them soon move over to the East Coast.

On 9 April 1958, D200 worked a test train from Doncaster to Welwyn and return. Initially allocated to Stratford, one example, D201, was transferred to Hornsey on 25 April for testing and driver training, working some Cambridge and Grantham services. On 21 June 1958, the loco made its first appearance on the down 'Flying Scotsman', at the time booked non-stop to Newcastle in five hours and one minute, a leisurely start to stop average of 53.4mph over the 268 miles.

The diesels allocated for ECML work were D201 and D206–09, later to become 40001 and 40006–09. With no available space at King's Cross shed, the new machines were allocated to Hornsey. With

An unidentified Deltic is seen near Hitchin on 1A15, the up 'Tees-Tyne Pullman' (09.20 from Newcastle) on 5 October 1964. (Through Their Eyes)

55014 *The Duke of Wellington's Regiment* **departs King's Cross on 3 August 1975. (Trevor Ermel)**

the success of these early trials, the five Hornsey machines took over the 'Tees-Tyne' and 'Sheffield Pullman' services and the 'Flying Scotsman' from the winter timetable onwards.

With the new diesels having some teething problems, steam was still found standing in for the new locos in the early 1960s. With trains still timed for steam, there was no knock-on effect on punctuality, although the shorter turnaround times scheduled for diesels did cause some issues at the termini.

There were 56 examples of the Class 46s built between 1961 and 1963 at British Railways' Derby Works. Initially numbered D138–93, they were viewed by some as a forerunner of the Class 47s, with similar electrical equipment and power unit. Initially, a further 20 Class 46s were ordered but this was cancelled in favour of the new Brush Type 4s, which went on to be D1500–19.

Class 46s were very regular performers on the ECML, particularly between Newcastle and York on cross-country duties (Gateshead and Laira-allocated examples) and trans-Pennine and secondary East Coast services (mostly Gateshead-allocated examples). The Class 46 fleet provided sterling and reliable service, but a lack of electric train heating (ETH) saw them removed from East Coast passenger duties and the influx of Type 5 diesels saw their freight duties dry up too, with the whole class withdrawn by the end of 1984.

The 512 examples of the Class 47 were built by Brush Traction at Loughborough and by BR at Crewe Works between 1962 and 1968, and they went on to be the standard Type 4, operating a wide variety of freight and passenger services all over the network. The initial build of 20 locomotives (D1500–19, later 47401–20 and dubbed 'Generators') used Westinghouse-supplied brake systems, rather than the later standard Metcalfe-Oerlikon brakes, and were withdrawn earlier than the rest of the class (from 1986) because of their non-standard nature.

D9004 (later 55004 *Queen's Own Highlander*) passes through Northallerton on 19 April 1963 on 1A39, a Glasgow to King's Cross service. (Andy Flowers Collection)

55019 *Royal Highland Fusilier* at Newcastle on 1V93, the 09.50 Edinburgh–Plymouth, with 50010 *Monarch* on the Doncaster test train after release from 'The Plant'. (Trevor Ermel)

In August 1962, an unidentified Class 45 approaches Newark on 1N19, the 13.15 King's Cross to Leeds/Halifax. (Andy Flowers Collection)

On 25 February 1983, Class 40 40180 makes a colourful sight at King's Cross on 3S35, the 14.10 parcels service for Edinburgh Waverley. (Andy Flowers Collection)

Other dual-heat Class 47 locomotives were allocated to the Eastern Region and proved their worth on the East Coast, being able to haul air-conditioned and electrically heated stock during the day and steam heat-only Mk.1 sleepers and coaches on overnight services. Class 47s were the last class of diesel loco allocated to daytime loco-hauled express services on the East Coast, ending in the early 1990s, and also the overnight 'Nightrider' trains. The class were also the last locos rostered for the Newcastle to Liverpool Trans-Pennine services.

The English Electric Company decided in the 1950s to develop a diesel electric locomotive with a high power/weight ratio with the prototype Deltic introduced in 1955. The Napier power unit was also used in ten Type 2 Bo-Bos, the Class 23 Baby Deltics.

In 1959, the prototype Deltic (DP1) began testing on the ECML, initially entering service between King's Cross and Doncaster only. The Deltic prototype gave a significant improvement in performance over the Pacific steam locos handling British Railways' heaviest and fastest passenger services at the time.

The ER later ordered 23 locos for its top express work, later cutting the order to 22. With their higher speed, availability and quicker turnaround times, the 22 Deltics were able to replace 55 Pacifics. The production Deltics were different in design to DP1, being seven tons lighter, 3ft 6in longer and with a narrower profile to improve clearances and with an attractive two-tone green livery.

The remaining Class 40s still on top-link work were soon replaced by Deltics on most of the prime duties, with regular timetabled operation beginning on 1 June 1961. The whole fleet was delivered between February 1961 and April 1962 and were initially allocated as follows:

- Finsbury Park: D9001/03/07/09/12/15/18/20.
- Gateshead: D9002/05/08/11/14/17.
- Haymarket: D9000/04/06/10/13/16/19/21.

D9003 *Meld* heads through Selby on 2 March 1963 on a Glasgow to King's Cross service, with DMUs for Hull to the left and Goole to the right. (Andy Flowers Collection)

Main Line Diesel Locomotives

To enable operation with Mk.2 stock, introduced in the 1960s, the class was fitted with train air brakes in 1967/68 and ETH at Doncaster from 1970 onwards.

On 2 February 1978, 55008 was given the chance to display the type's high-speed potential on the 07.25 Newcastle to King's Cross, a train with a retiring driver, some well-informed train timing experts on board and some record-breaking speeds. With a load of ten coaches, the Deltic achieved a net average speed of 97mph start to stop with a maximum of 113mph between Darlington and York and an amazing 125mph down Stoke Bank, almost matching the world record breaking achievements of *Mallard*. It has been estimated that with today's improved infrastructure, including the Selby Diversion, a sub-five hours 'Flying Scotsman' schedule would be possible with a Deltic.

Apart from their core King's Cross–Edinburgh duties, the Deltics, particularly in their later years, worked a number of secondary East Coast services, including semi-fasts to York and duties to locations including Cleethorpes and Aberdeen, with rarer trips to Skegness and Scarborough. The class also began to be used on Trans-Pennine services to Liverpool, particularly locos restricted to one working power unit.

The Deltics began to lose the top-link work on the East Coast upon introduction of the HSTs in 1978. The last Deltic run on a service train took place on 31 December 1981, with 55019 on the 16.30 Aberdeen–York, taking the train forward from Edinburgh. The final railtour on 2 January 1982 saw 55015 work the special from London to Edinburgh and 55022 return it to King's Cross. The remaining intact Deltics were sent to Doncaster for disposal or sale to preservationists, six being eventually restored.

Some thought had been given to moving the Deltic fleet to the Midland Main Line to replace the Class 45/1s there (before the introduction of HSTs), or even to the North East-South West corridor. However, increasing maintenance costs, added to the high cost of the required crew training, saw the fleet withdrawn.

D9021 *Argyll and Sutherland Highlander* **near Low Fell on the up 'Flying Scotsman' on 29 April 1967. (Trevor Ermel)**

Main Line Diesel Locomotives

55015 *Tulyar* **stands next to 40084 at Newcastle with both locos on overnight workings for London in December 1979. (Andy Flowers Collection)**

55017 *The Durham Light Infantry* **passes through Wood Green on 1 August 1978. (Trevor Ermel)**

On 18 October 1997, D9000 Royal Scots Grey stands at King's Cross on the 'Trans-Pennine Deltic Lament' railtour.

On 17 December 2021, 68020 prepares to shove a Mark 5 set towards Scarborough. TPE services, including these 'Nova 3' sets, travel along the shared trackbed next to the ECML between York and Colton Junction, and may become the only remaining regularly scheduled loco-hauled trains over the entire East Coast route.

Chapter 12
King's Cross Suburban Diesels

BR struggled to replace pre-grouping steam locos, including the much-loved N2s (with some L1s and B1s), with diesel traction on the suburban services. At the beginning of 1959, 40 new diesels and a number of DMUs were allocated to Great Northern suburban services with the intention of withdrawing steam on the commuter routes out of Broad Street, Moorgate and King's Cross.

The locos included 20 Class 26s, ten Class 21s and ten Class 23s. The Class 26s aside, the new locos proved very unreliable, and steam soldiered on until at least 1962 on a number of services. Other exotic classes featured on these services in the early years included Class 15s, 16s and 20s.

Class 26s D5300–D5309 (26001–09/20) were delivered new to Hornsey depot between 1958 and 1959, and some members of the class were based there until October 1960. They were used regularly on commuter services out of King's Cross to Hertford North, Hitchin and Welwyn. The locos were also used out of Moorgate from 1 December 1958. The type was also reported on a number of longer distance services, including D5300 (26007) on a King's Cross to Grimsby train on 20 June 1959.

Baby Deltic D5901 stands at King's Cross on 1B66, the famous 17.34 King's Cross–Cambridge 'Buffet Express', in January 1965. (Andy Flowers Collection)

Baby Deltic D5901 arrives at Hornsey on a commuter working from King's Cross on 12 June 1961. (Andy Flowers Collection)

Class 24 D5033 (later 24033) leaves King's Cross in January 1962 with empty coaching stock from a local suburban stopping service. (Andy Flowers Collection)

North British Class 21s worked Great Northern commuter trains out of King's Cross after being allocated to Hornsey from 1958. By March 1960, the class had proven so chronically unreliable that they were placed in store at New England Yard, Peterborough, and/or sent to Eastfield.

In the case of the BTH Class 15s and NBL Class 16s, these low-powered Type 1s did not possess train heating boilers and only saw use in the summer months or during periods of low availability for the more powerful, and more reliable, Type 2s. With only ten of the Class 16s compared to the 44 Class 15s, and the BTH locos being marginally more reliable, the latter were more common passenger performers, with D8232 reported on the 17.41 Moorgate to Hartford as late as 8 May 1969.

The introduction of the Brush Type 2s from 1960 (these Class 30s were later to become Class 31s after re-engining) together with 25 Class 24s from the London Midland Region saw the transfer away to Scotland of the Class 21s and Class 26s and Class 20s being moved almost exclusively on to freight duties. In 1968, the Class 24s moved on to pastures new while the Baby Deltics continued largely on Broad Street duties until the introduction of further DMUs in 1969.

Class 47s, somewhat overpowered for the role, were also used in the mid-1960s on some Quad-Art sets, notably working from Welwyn Garden City to King's Cross in 1966.

By the late 1960s, Class 31s were the core motive power for inner suburban commuter services on the former GNR lines. The type continued on these services, including workings out of Moorgate to Welwyn Garden City, up until electrification in 1976. Electrification of the inner GN lines from 1971 to 1978 (as far as Royston) put an end to diesel-hauled suburban commuter trains out of London, including the King's Cross–Cambridge buffet expresses.

Cambridge Expresses

In the diesel era, the Cambridge Express services were worked by a wide variety of motive power. Running every two hours with a 1B66 reporting number, the trains comprised seven or eight Mk.1s, including a Gresley-designed buffet, giving the services the term 'The Cambridge Buffet Expresses'. Some services also started and terminated at Baldock (north of Stevenage). The services were stopped after electrification through to Cambridge in 1978 with 47100 working the final 1B66 19.30 King's Cross–Cambridge on Sunday 5 February, complete with commemorative headboard. In the 1960s, everything from a Class 20 to a Deltic worked the Cambridge trains, the full list of types comprising:

- Class 20 (generally only following failures)
- Class 21
- Class 23 Baby Deltics
- Class 24
- Class 26
- Class 31 (the most common form of diesel motive power, occasionally in pairs)
- Class 37 (rare, a handful of appearances following failures)
- Class 40
- Class 46
- Class 47
- Class 55 Deltics (occasionally turned out, often examples on just one power unit)
- D0260 *Lion* (unconfirmed)
- DP2 (used on occasional fill in turns)
- D0280 *Falcon*

Chapter 13
Prototypes and Occasional Passenger Locos

Other than the well-reviewed express locos on the ECML, such as the Deltics and Class 91s, a large number of smaller classes have performed over sections of the route, starting with the introduction of diesels on the London inner and outer suburban services in the late 1950s, as detailed above.

With the ECML's reputation for high-speed running, it has been a very useful testbed over the years to trial new high-speed locomotives, a use that was upheld in the early years of the introduction of diesels on the main line. Prototypes trialled included DP1 (prototype Deltic), DP2 (prototype Class 50), HS4000 *Kestrel* and the trial Type 4 locos *Falcon* and *Lion*. The 'Master Cutler' and 'Sheffield Pullman' were particularly useful trains for testing diesel prototypes out of King's Cross in the early 1960s, with DP2, *Falcon* and *Lion* all seeing use on these services.

DP1 (Diesel Prototype 1) was the first of the experimental high-powered diesel locos tested by British Railways in the 1950s and 1960s with a view to follow-on orders. It soon showed the potential for high speed and acceleration of services up to regular 100mph running. After a spell on the WCML, DP1 soon settled down on King's Cross–Leeds/Doncaster services, and it was while on one of these services it suffered a major failure at Doncaster in March 1961 and was withdrawn, and then donated to the Science Museum in London. The success of the design led to an order for the production Deltics.

DP2 was built in 1962 as a test bed for the later Class 50s, although using a Deltic-style bodyshell. The 2,700hp 16CSVT power unit proved very reliable, and despite having lower installed horsepower

DP2 arrives at King's Cross at the head of the up 'Sheffield Pullman' in April 1964. (Through Their Eyes)

than a Deltic and a top speed of only 90mph, DP2 managed to keep Deltic schedules on many services upon transfer to Finsbury Park in July 1963, including King's Cross–Edinburgh diagrams. A particular favourite diagram was an overnight King's Cross–York train, returning in the morning, then taking two return trips to Cambridge. DP2 was withdrawn after a collision with the Cliffe–Uddingston cement service at Thirsk on 31 July 1967.

D0260 *Lion* was a prototype Type 4 main line diesel-electric locomotive built in 1962 by a consortium of the Birmingham Railway Carriage and Wagon Company (BRC&W), Sulzer the engine maker and Associated Electrical Industries at BRC&W's Smethwick Works. Using a standard Sulzer 12LDA28-C power unit rated at 2,750hp, the loco had a top speed of 100mph. The loco saw use out of King's Cross, mostly on the 'Sheffield Pullman', during 1963–64 but also on some Leeds services and, reportedly, a Cambridge turn. It suffered a flashover while working a Sheffield service in 1964 and was withdrawn, as BR had by then ordered its Type 4 fleet from Brush.

D0280 *Falcon* was built as a demonstrator by Brush in 1961 using two Maybach MD655 power units rated at 2880hp in total, giving a top speed of 100mph. BR classified the prototype as a Class 53 and it was based at Finsbury Park from 1961, working a number of passenger services, particularly the Cambridge Expresses and also the 'Sheffield Pullman' throughout 1962 and 1963. Despite being non-standard, the loco proved very reliable and lasted in service on the Western Region until 1975, after transfer in 1965.

HS4000 *Kestrel* was a one-off prototype built by Brush in collaboration with Hawker Siddeley in 1967, with a view to follow-on orders and displaying a variety of advanced technological features. Its Sulzer 16LVA24 engine was rated at 4,000hp and gave a design speed of 125mph. Unfortunately, the design of power unit led to a crippling overall weight of 133t, which saw the loco restricted to freight use in its early days in traffic.

With new Class 47 bogies fitted, the axle weight was lowered sufficiently to enable high speed running, although the new bogies and smaller motors meant that the power output had to be lowered to 3,775hp. *Kestrel* was put into service with a regular diagram in lieu of a Deltic on King's Cross–Newcastle services in 1969, and the loco was timed hauling a ten-coach service up Stoke Bank at

HS4000 *Kestrel* crosses Durham Viaduct on 1 November 1969 on 1N08, a King's Cross to Newcastle working. (Trevor Ermel)

99mph. Reportedly, the loco was capable of beating Deltic timings with ease, being a full 14 minutes quicker over the Newcastle run.

Unfortunately, the loco was still too heavy, despite modifications, and after its maximum speed was reduced to 75mph, it saw restricted use and was taken off passenger use after the end of 1969. There are few reliable logs of *Kestrel* reaching 125mph in service, although footage of it on test with the speedometer levelled at 110mph for sustained periods demonstrate that it had the potential for very high-speed running.

As a development of the Deltics and DP2, a Super Deltic (Class 51) was proposed, with three possible power ratings between 4,000 and 4,600hp and with a bodyshell similar to the Class 50. The power units would have been two 18-cylinder turbo-charged Napiers, enabling the axle weight to be kept below 20t. The design never saw the light of day but could have accelerated services significantly before the introduction of the HSTs in the late 1970s.

Although not locos, the use of GWR diesel railcar No.19, together with (reportedly) Nos. 6 or 8, and 11, on trials on loan to the LNER in the Newcastle area in 1944 is worthy of note. Details of the workings are sketchy, no doubt due to wartime restrictions, although No.19 was noted at Blackhill on the Derwent Valley Railway (from Newcastle to Consett via Swalwell) in April 1944.

The Class 17s were perhaps the least successful of the early main line diesel types ordered by BR, in many instances lasting only around five years in service. Despite their low speed, low power, lack of train heat and poor reliability, they were occasionally trusted on passenger services. While there appears to be no recorded instances of Class 17s appearing on the ECML, while some of the type were shedded at Haymarket and Gateshead, it is highly likely that they appeared on a few local duties or excursions, particularly the Haymarket-based examples, which were noted on regular forays on passenger trains to Carstairs.

With a top speed of only 75mph, Class 20s were not a common sight on the ECML although early in their life some members of the class were allocated to Hornsey shed from 1959, replacing Class 26s. The locos worked alongside Classes 21, 23 and 30 on stopping trains to Baldock on the Cambridge line, Ely and Hitchin and branches off the main line, including Hatfield to Dunstable North (closed to passengers in 1965). The 20s were reallocated to Finsbury Park in 1960 and remained there for two more years. They were not unknown on King's Cross to Cambridge services, deputising for failed Baby Deltics.

On 31 August 1986, 20013 and 20047 worked the 10.18 Scarborough to Newcastle throughout, a rare run down the ECML for the type on a Class 1 passenger service. Another notable working was single 20155 on 2 February 1986 rescuing the 23.35 King's Cross–Aberdeen sleeper at Tallington (north of Peterborough) and working the train forward to Grantham.

Class 23 Baby Deltics were used primarily on King's Cross inner suburban duties and also on Cambridge services but occasionally worked as far north as Peterborough on commuter trains. They proved spectacularly unsuccessful.

Other than initially working commuter traffic out of King's Cross and Moorgate, Sulzer Type 2 workings on the ECML were uncommon in later years, but in the 1960s they made regular appearances in the northeast. By the end of 1960, Class 24s were diagrammed between Newcastle and Edinburgh on the 'Heart of Midlothian' service (King's Cross–Edinburgh). Gateshead had an allocation of Class 24s between 1960 and 1974, these making appearances on Newcastle–Leeds trains and a number of York–Glasgow reliefs, and also Class 25s between 1963 and 1974 working similar services.

With the arrival of Deltics and Class 47s by 1963, the northeastern-based Type 2s lost almost all their passenger duties on the ECML, with only local services to Edinburgh, along the Tyne Valley and

31203 stands at King's Cross with empty stock on 29 April 1978 with an unidentified Class 47 and Deltic on service trains. (Andy Flowers Collection)

31405 and 31198 pass Abbots Ripton (north of Huntingdon) with a mixed parcels service for King's Cross on 17 March 1980. (Andy Flowers Collection)

occasional relief services to the Manchester area being reported. A notable working was D7573 (later 25223) on the 08.25 Leeds to King's Cross on 13 January 1968.

In the 1970s and early 1980s, Class 24s (up until 1976), 25s and 26s were noted on Edinburgh–Newcastle–Carlisle stopping services and one-off workings on inter-regionals between Newcastle and York, particularly the 07.30 Birmingham–Newcastle service. One particularly rare working was 25278, on 13 June 1984, with an evening Newcastle to Durham working. Class 25s were also used to haul the Royal train over East Coast metals on a number of occasions.

Class 25s made occasional appearances on the King's Cross to Peterborough commuter services until the 1980s, particularly on the 06.32 and 08.03 Peterborough–King's Cross workings. This included a '24/25' combination on 2 August 1973, with 5190 and 7608 and a number of '31/25' combinations, including 31185 and 25037 on the 06.43 Peterborough–King's Cross on 12 March 1973, and 31108 and 25085 on the same train on 5 November 1974.

On 19 August 1975, 25081 took over a 13.30 Newcastle–King's Cross relief at Peterborough after the failure of 47177. On 9 January 1979, 25074 and 31408 worked the 07.08 Peterborough–King's Cross. A rare late visitor to King's Cross in the career of the Class 25s was 25037, which was paired with 31185 on the 06.43 from Peterborough on 12 March 1981.

In the early 1970s, the 14.15 Edinburgh–Newcastle stopping service was frequently hauled by Haymarket Type 2s of Classes 24, 26 or 27. This train ran with Type 2s until the end of 1975. Class 26s and Class 27s were also very occasional performers on East Coast overnight trains to and from Newcastle. In 1975, 26004 worked the 17.10 Edinburgh–Newcastle stopping service on July 18. On 14 August 1975, BR ran what was effectively a railtour with a relief to the 20.15 King's Cross–Edinburgh, this starting at Peterborough owing to heavy rain the London area and featuring 31214 as far as Newcastle and 26001 forward to Edinburgh.

40058 stands at King's Cross with the 23.49 parcels service for Newcastle on 23 December 1982.

With its distinctive cut-away bodyside exposing drainage piping, 40069 sits steaming away at King's Cross at midnight at the start of Christmas Eve in 1982 with 1N20, the 00.05 to Newcastle. This train was a good bet for a Class 40 at the time and was one of the author's particular favourite night's out.

On 21 December 1978, 26024 worked an Aberdeen to Newcastle relief service, heading back to Edinburgh on another relief. 26014 and 26031 featured on the 20.35 Aberdeen–King's Cross as far as Newcastle on 31 August 1979, heading back north across the border on the 23.15 King's Cross to Edinburgh. On 22 August 1984, 27001 worked the 13.00 King's Cross–Dundee forward from Newcastle in place of an unavailable Class 47. On 21 December 1978, 26024 worked an Aberdeen to Newcastle relief train throughout, returning with another relief to Edinburgh.

The cross-country Leicester to Peterborough service featured Class 27s until June 1966, bringing the Type 2s onto the southern stretches of the ECML. After their transfer to Scotland, Class 27s were regular performers on a morning commuter service from Dunbar into Edinburgh. On 25 February 1979, 27019 worked an Aviemore–Newcastle special, heading back north on the 20.00 King's Cross–Aberdeen.

Another rare southern outing for the class took place on 1 September 1981, when 27105 and 27110 stood in for an unavailable HST set on the 08.36 Aberdeen–King's Cross service. The Class 27s worked over the East Coast as far as Newcastle, where the train was terminated, the locos and stock returning north empty. The following year, on 6 August, 27016 also made it as far as Newcastle on the 21.05 Edinburgh–King's Cross, heading back north the next day on the 19.01 King's Cross–Aberdeen parcels service.

On 17 October 1982, the 21.40 Glasgow–Nottingham was diverted over the Tyne Valley line with a Class 27 working through to Newcastle again, this time in the shape of 27004. On 22 August 1984, 27001 worked forward from Newcastle on the 11.00 King's Cross–Dundee.

On Saturday 10 July 2010, 33207 waits to leave York on a railtour to Whitby with 37676 at the rear. The low morning sun highlights the spectacular lighting effects sometimes seen from the original NER overall roof. A fine run was had with the Crompton down the ECML.

On 5 June 1981, 40170 passes through York on the famous Red Bank empties, this being the 5M48 09.38 Heaton (Newcastle) to Red Bank (Manchester), which was the return of the previous evening's newspaper service from Manchester. (Andy Flowers Collection)

Apart from their core Great Northern commuter role, Class 31s shared 'Sheffield Pullman' and Cleethorpes duties into King's Cross with Class 37s in the early 1960s. The type also worked a 12.00 Newcastle–Lincoln service as late as 1969. From the 1970s, the class went on to appear on Peterborough–King's Cross commuter services and right up to the 1980s, featured occasionally on overnight sleeper services, particularly to and from Leeds.

Some particularly rare appearances by Class 31s across the border took place on the 17.10 Edinburgh to Newcastle stopper, which featured 31162 on 18 July 1978 and 31158 on 10 March 1979. Class 31s are also known to have appeared as far north as Edinburgh after rescuing Type 4s on sleeper services and some Class 31/4s were reported on Newcastle–Liverpool services.

With Class 33s being restricted to the Southern Region for most of their lives, save for a short period later in their careers with forays into Wales and the northwest, there have been few opportunities for passenger work on the ECML, although they have been occasional visitors on empty stock, charters and railtours.

While passenger use for Class 33s was rare on the East Coast, there was one famous freight working, the 02.30 Holborough (Cliffe) to Uddingston and 02.45 return cement train. This heavy train generally loaded to 28 wagons and was booked for a pair of 33s as far as York, with a Class 40 working forward. The train ran from 4 December 1961 until October 1976. The Class 33s occasionally ran light engine back to the Southern Region, and while it is possible that they may have rescued failed services while heading back south, there are no confirmed reports. A number of Class 33s were loaned to the Eastern Region for training for this duty, including D6504 and D6559 to Finsbury Park in 1961 and D6556, D6517, D6559, D6541 and D6553 to New England between 1961 and 1963.

In connection with WCML electrification in the early 1960s, BR experimented with applying electric train heating to its Mk.1 stock. As part of this programme, D6504 (33004) hauled a test train formed of eight modified coaches from Derby to Peterborough and King's Cross on 10 February 1961. The stock

DRS-liveried 33025, complete with its short-lived 'Mini-modal' branding, approaches Colton Junction in August 2002 with a West Coast Railways empty stock movement to York with 57601 bringing up the rear. Until privatisation, the sight of Class 33s on hauled stock on the ECML approaching York would have been restricted to one-off railtour duties. (Andy Flowers Collection)

was then used on overnight tests between King's Cross and Craigentinny on the 14th and 16th, running back south on the 15th and 17th. The Class 33 was worked by King's Cross crews, who regularly drove the class on the Uddingston cements, with a pilotman on board north of York.

From 1975 onwards, Class 33s began to make appearances for the annual flower show at Spalding, traversing the ECML between London and Peterborough en route. On 10 May, two specials arrived from Ramsgate, one featuring 33041, the other reportedly hauled by 33046. On 6 May 1978, 33034 worked through from Brighton and 33035 from Dover Priory. In 1977, a Brighton–Peterborough football special was worked by 33057 throughout and 33015 worked a similar train through to Lincoln on 20 April.

In March 1984, before the introduction of the locomotive-hauled Gatwick Express services, one of the soon to be introduced trains was sent on a nationwide promotional tour. This saw 33113 and Mk.2f-based sets 8201 and 8306 travel from Stewarts Lane to Newcastle via Chester, Manchester and Sheffield. After stabling overnight at Heaton on 15 March, the loco and stock returned back south the next day.

Perhaps the highest profile Class 33 railtour to work over the ECML took place on 16 March 1996, when 33109 and 33116 worked the 'Skirl o' the Bagpipes 2', from King's Cross to Aberdeen. The following year on 22 March 1997, 33051 and 33116 worked from King's Cross to Skegness, out via the East Midlands but returning via the East Coast direct via Grantham. In the same year, on 14 June, the 'Whitby Jet' railtour ran from King's Cross to Whitby with 33030 and 33116.

The only true timetabled passenger working for a Class 33 anywhere near the ECML took place on the extension to Aberdeen. Following privatisation, EWS outbased a handful of Class 33s at Aberdeen for local freight workings and shunting duties. On 10 October 2000, 33030 was provided for 1B16, the Aberdeen portion of the Euston sleeper service following the failure of 47732.

West Coast Railways Class 33s have worked a number of charters and empty coaching stock workings over the East Coast with the possibility of further appearances in the future, with the company still owning three working examples.

37072 stands at York on 16 July 1977, working the 11.25 Edinburgh to King's Cross after rescuing a Deltic at Darlington. The badly dressed gaggle of trainspotters appear disinterested, despite the rarity of the working. (Andy Flowers Collection)

Class 37s were not unknown at King's Cross, featuring on the 'Sheffield Pullman' in 1963 and on some King's Cross to Cleethorpes and Hull trains in the same year. They were also reported occasionally on commuter trains between King's Cross and Peterborough, and they were known to work cross-country services between Newcastle–York, and the Great Yarmouth–Newcastle summer-dated services to and from Peterborough. However, the class was rare on longer distance East Coast express trains into and out of the London terminus.

On Saturday 22 October 1983, Western Region-allocated 37180 was diagrammed to work an 08.27 Leeds to King's Cross relief with a rake of 90mph-limited Mk.1s. The loco also worked a 14.03 King's Cross–Newcastle relief back northwards, but after an excellent performance by the Type 3, the train was terminated at Peterborough with hot boxes due to sustained 100mph running with smoke visibly pouring out of the bogies along the train. Class 37s were also noted on a number of other relief services into and out of King's Cross in the early 1980s and occasionally deputising for Type 4s or Deltics that had failed or were unavailable.

Class 45s were frequent visitors to King's Cross in the 1960s, their appearances becoming less commonplace throughout the 1970s, although still seeing Holbeck-allocated examples working King's Cross to Leeds and Bradford trains. By the 1980s, their appearances were only occasional, with one of the last visits noted being 45012 on 21 April 1986 after rescuing a failed 47523 on an overnight service from Aberdeen.

On 28 May 1975, Holbeck's 45036 was noted working an overnight service to Aberdeen, and on 3 June the same year, 45134 arrived from Newcastle and worked back north with a service to Leeds. Class 45/1s were also diverted into King's Cross in 1981 from St Pancras due to engineering works.

The appearance of Western Region-allocated Class 37 37180 *Sir Dyfed/County of Dyfed* **at King's Cross on 22 October 1983 caused a level of consternation amongst traincrew and platform staff, as seen here. The loco had arrived at 'The Cross' earlier in the day from Leeds and is seen here on the 14.03 relief to Newcastle.**

Gateshead-allocated Class 46s were more generally used in preference to Class 45s on overnight and daytime steam-heated semi-fast services and reliefs.

Some of the rarest workings for diesels on passenger turns on the East Coast were by Class 50s, released after overhaul and refurbishment at Doncaster Works between 1977 and 1987. Highly notable was 50009, which, on 10 June 1977, made the debut for the class at King's Cross, arriving with 1A10, the 08.36 from Hull, after taking over the train at Doncaster. The loco returned north on 1L20, the 14.10 to Leeds. In later years, Class 50s tended to be sent back west from York on an Edinburgh to Penzance service, although a very notable working took place on 8 April 1982, when 50030 worked the 06.20 Cleethorpes to King's Cross throughout.

Western Region diesel hydraulics were not seen on the ECML save for railtour duties. On 10 April 1965, Hymek D7060 worked a Weymouth to Cambridge football excursion, although this passed across the ECML, working via Oxford and Bedford. At least one Western (D1008 in 1965) made it to Cambridge on another excursion, routed the same way.

D1023 *Western Fusilier* made the debut for the class out of King's Cross on 20 November 1976 with the 'Western Talisman' railtour to York. Fast forward to 2008, and on 3 May, mainline-certified D1015 *Western Champion* worked a tour between Newcastle and Edinburgh. On 5 December 2009, D1015 worked from King's Cross to York and return with the 'White Rose' railtour, commemorating the run with D1023 some 33 years earlier.

In January 2007, a Riviera Trains standby rake of Mk.2 coaches formed a service from Birmingham New Street to Newcastle hauled by a Class 57/3. This sub-class, along with 57601, have also made occasional appearances on the ECML on tours and charters, particularly the 'Northern Belle'.

Type 5 diesels have rarely been seen on passenger duties on the East Coast due to their low top speed (60-80mph) and lack of train heat provision. Railtours have seen Classes 56, 58, 60 and 66 make

Another view of 37180 on the ECML on Saturday 22 October 1983 on the 08.27 relief service from Leeds to King's Cross, this time at Peterborough.

Prototypes and Occasional Passenger Locos

37221 heads through Doncaster in 1978 after rescuing 47513 just south of the station on a service from King's Cross to Edinburgh. (Andy Flowers Collection)

occasional appearances over part of the route, but in terms of service trains, only Class 56s and 66s have made appearances following rescues of failed locos.

In June 1985, 56115 rescued 47423 at Ouston Junction on a Newcastle–Liverpool service and reportedly dragged the train as far as York. 56122 also came to the rescue of 45141 near Durham after it failed on a Poole–Newcastle service in April 1988. 56128 was reported as assisting a failing 47401 *North Eastern* on 17 September 1985, piloting the previous night's 20.35 from Aberdeen forward from Doncaster to the London terminus.

Class 58s were seen on Doncaster to Peterborough test trains as part of their commissioning process, using stock formed of Mk.2s but unfortunately running as empty stock. Class 58s also made a couple of appearances at King's Cross on railtours, both to Skegness. The first outing featured 58039 on 20 September 1986 with 58024 out and 58020 back on the 'Bone Idol' on 1 September 2002. This was the final passenger working for the class, the remaining three examples being switched off at Old Oak Common two days later.

60017 made an unexpected foray to King's Cross on a railtour on 11 June 2016 following the failure of train loco 60163 *Tornado* at York. Class 66s have been reported rescuing a number of HST sets in the last two decades, with at least one example also appearing on a cross-country service, 66162 rescuing 67001 at Wakefield Westgate on 1E99, the 09.05 Paignton–Newcastle service on 31 July 2004. This was also reportedly the last time a locomotive from Healey Mills depot was despatched to work a timetabled passenger service.

Class 67s took over from Class 47s on Thunderbird rescue duties from May 2003, being based at King's Cross, Doncaster, Newcastle and Edinburgh. The new National Express franchise shortly afterwards saw the Class 67 Thunderbird fleet increase from four to five, with the extra loco to be based at Peterborough.

67017 at Newcastle on Sunday 8 February 2004 on the 08.30 Doncaster–Glasgow Central after arrival, having dragging 91106 *East Lothian* from York.

On 20 February 2007, 67028 has arrived at Newark as a security guard walks down the platform to needlessly harass the photographer.

67026 stands at Leeds on 15 January 2012 on 1A43, the 16.45 Leeds–King's Cross, dragging 91121.

On 5 February 2017, 67022 stands at the bufferstops at King's Cross after dragging 1Y14, the 08.00 York–King's Cross, from Peterborough via Cambridge. Cambridge has historically been a well-used diversionary route for East Coast services during weekend engineering work.

Since then, the class has featured regularly on planned and emergency passenger work on the East Coast, dragging Class 91s and Mk.4 stock over diversionary routes or during overhead power shutdowns, but also due to the occasional failure of the electric loco. This rescue work should end with the final withdrawal of the Class 91 and Mk.4 sets. In 2004, Virgin CrossCountry also hired a number of Class 67s for Newcastle to Paignton summer Saturday trains.

68008 made the debut for the Class 68s at King's Cross on 8 August 2015, working the Inverness-bound 'Northern Belle' as far as Edinburgh. TransPennine Express Class 68s work over the ECML between York and Colton Junction on services between Liverpool/Manchester and York/Scarborough.

Using a Deltic Well away from its more familiar ECML stomping ground, between 1997 and 1999, Virgin Trains (CrossCountry) was a regular user of D9000 (55022) *Royal Scots Grey,* **the loco having a regular summer Saturday-only turn from Birmingham New Street to Ramsgate and return. On 25 July 1998, D9000 arrives at Coventry on 1O99, the 6.58 Birmingham New Street to Ramsgate.**

Chapter 14

High Speed Trains

The prototype High Speed Train, which was designated as a Class 252 DEMU at the time, started trials on the ECML in mid-1973. It achieved a BR speed record at the time of 131mph between Northallerton and Thirsk. The set was planned to enter service on the Leeds–Edinburgh 'North Briton' but never appeared due to a dispute with the unions over double-manning. Nevertheless, it created another diesel speed record (this time a world record) on 11 June 1973, reaching 143mph on 12 June 1973. This was later beaten by 43102 (now 43302) and 43159, which set the world record for diesel traction on rail with 148.5mph on 1 November 1987 between Northallerton and York, again on test.

The first East Coast HST run was a press demonstration special from King's Cross to Peterborough on 26 April 1977. The first timetabled HST ran on 20 March 1978 on the 07.45 King's Cross–Edinburgh and 15.00 return. On 8 May 1978, the first HSTs began entering squadron service on the ECML initially with six sets, four on King's Cross–Edinburgh workings and two on Newcastle trains. By 1979, this had increased to 32 daily services.

SC43086 (part of set 254016) passes through York on 31 May 1978. The power car was new to traffic only two days earlier and is seen here on a test run. (Trevor Ermel)

43312 (with 43039 at the rear) approaches Newark North Gate on 15 January 2012 on a York to King's Cross service.

An HST with power cars 43088 and 43165 passes Dringhouses (just south of York) on 18 August 1998, working a King's Cross to Newcastle service. (Andy Flowers Collection)

43308 *Highland Chieftain* powers out of Doncaster on an Aberdeen–King's Cross service on 26 April 2018. 43309 was at the front of the train.

254022 stands at Leeds in August 1981 on a service for King's Cross. (Andy Flowers Collection)

On 15 November 2008, a HST owned by open access operator Grand Central prepares to leave King's Cross for Sunderland, with 43123 leading.

Following many years of excellent performance, accessibility regulations meant that the HST fleet needed to be withdrawn from East Coast services by the end of 2019.

Final LNER HST fleet (2019)

HST power cars, Angel Trains owned: 43206, 43208, 43238, 43239, 43295, 43296, 43305, 43306, 43307, 43308, 43309, 43310, 43311, 43312, 43313, 43314, 43315, 43316, 43317, 43318, 43319, 43320, 43367.

HST power cars, Porterbrook owned: 43251, 4257, 43272, 43274, 43290, 43299, 43300, 43202.

Withdrawn from ECML service following the full introduction of the Azuma fleet, some of the withdrawn HSTs have seen service in other areas. HST Class 43 power car 43277 is seen stored at Arely (Severn Valley Railway) on 26 September 2021. 43227 now forms part of the Colas-owned fleet allocated for use on Network Rail test trains.

Chapter 15

Shunters

Class 08s were used at Edinburgh Waverley for a number of shunt moves on loaded passenger trains, in particular attaching the Glasgow portion of the summer Saturdays-only service to Scarborough. Around the same time, some substantive mileage was available at Doncaster, with the resident 08 dragging Leeds/Newcastle portions of King's Cross-bound trains north out of the station during marshalling of overnight services.

One of the most notable Class 08 passenger turns on the ECML took place on 21 February 1991, when overhead line damage (caused by a Class 313 EMU) between the tunnels at the entrance to King's Cross saw 08957 haul a full passenger train into the terminal. This had been powered by Class 91 91003 and headed by DVT 82221 with a service from Leeds.

55021 *Argyll and Sutherland Highlander* **is seen climbing Copenhagen Bank on 1 August 1978 on the down 'Flying Scotsman'. An unidentified Class 08 is seen shunting a mixed freight in the background. (Trevor Ermel)**

Chapter 16

Electric Locomotives

The ECML was electrified in stages between 1976 and 1991:

- King's Cross to Hitchin: 1976–78.
- Hitchin to Huntingdon: 1986.
- Huntingdon to Leeds: 1988.
- Doncaster to York: 1989.
- York to Edinburgh: 1991.

In addition to the core electric motive power of Class 91s, classes 86, 87, 90 and 92 have occasionally worked (planned or emergency) diverted Caledonian Sleeper trains over the ECML and also some charter traffic. Class 90s have also stood in for Class 91s for extended periods on a number of occasions on daytime services.

With the introduction of the Mk.5 sleeper coaches, which are capable of haulage only by dedicated Class 92s, the opportunities for the appearance of older electric locomotives on timetabled ECML services will become minimal.

In 2008, Hull Trains was suffering from low availability of its Class 222 DEMUs and borrowed 86101 and a rake of Mk.3 coaches hired in from Cargo-D to work a number of its services between King's Cross and Doncaster, giving the unique sight of a Class 86 into and out of King's Cross on a daytime timetabled passenger service. The original intention had been to drag the set using a DRS Class 47 between Doncaster and Hull, though this plan was shelved.

The solitary Class 89, 89001, propels a Leeds–King's Cross train through Welwyn Garden City on 2 June 1997. (Andy Flowers Collection)

The first working took place from Doncaster to London on Friday 11 January 2008, this service also being the first timetabled passenger train in the UK to be worked by a preserved AC electric loco. The loco worked a number of mainly weekend services between King's Cross and Doncaster until its last outing on 13 April before returning to its LNWR Crewe base. Rumours that First Capital Connect was also considering using Class 86s on King's Cross–Peterborough and Cambridge commuter services never came to fruition.

89001 had been a speculative build prototype designed by Brush to a BR specification and built at Crewe Works in 1986 with the hope of securing orders for freight and passenger work on the West and East Coast Main Lines. Brush had hoped that the type could take over from the ageing Class 86 fleet and be adopted as the standard loco for East Coast work. It was introduced in 1987 and initially allocated to Crewe Electric depot before transfer to ECML duties, moving initially to Hornsey and then eventually Bounds Green before starting work.

89001's first timetabled passenger train was the 17.25 King's Cross to Peterborough commuter service on 15 July 1988, and this went on to become a regular working. Later, it saw use on services to Leeds, becoming the first electric loco to work there, in August 1988, and also Bradford Foster Square. TDM multiple working and push-pull control was added in 1989, and by the following year, the loco was working a regular Leeds diagram, hauling one of two rakes of Mk.2f stock. After a series of failures, the loco was stored at Bounds Green for over a year before being officially withdrawn in July 1992.

The loco owed much of its bodyshell design to the Class 43 HST power cars and featured many electronic controls and TDM for push-pull working. In line with established practice learnt through high-speed electric locomotive operation abroad, it soon became clear that any orders for high-speed passenger locos would most likely be Bo-Bos, meaning that no follow-on orders materialised for the 89. The project did prove useful however as a testbed for many of the components in the Class 92 Channel Tunnel locos.

89001 was saved for preservation and moved to the Midland Railway Centre at Swanwick in 1994. Following Great North Eastern Railways' (GNER) award of the ECML franchise in 1996, the

Gresley A4 4468 *Mallard* leaves Doncaster on 3 July 1988 as part of the 50th anniversary celebrations of its 126mph record-breaking run. The train had arrived behind 89001, while 91003 is on display in the centre road in the distance, showing the future high-speed motive power for the line. (Andy Flowers Collection)

On 13 January 2008, 86101 leaves Doncaster for King's Cross on an up Hull Trains service, a rare use of a Class 86 on a timetabled ECML service.

89001 stands at Bounds Green with an unidentified Class 91 in August 1990. (Andy Flowers Collection)

train operator looked at options for motive power to help expand services on the route. The parent company, Sea Containers, was rumoured to have invested around £100,000 in buying the locomotive and restoring it for main line use. 89001 was returned to service in March 1997 by GNER for use on 110mph Leeds and Bradford trains, although the loco was clearly capable of higher speed running. The author personally timed 89001 at 132.5mph near Huntingdon on a late running up service in 2000.

91016 arrives at Leeds on a service from King's Cross in March 1996. (Andy Flowers Collection)

The loco needed only a few modifications during its overhaul by Brush at Loughborough before it could re-enter revenue earning service on GNER trains. After a year under repair at Loughborough (between autumn 1999 and late summer 2000) with bogie and traction motor issues, a major traction motor failure at the end of 2000 saw the loco finally withdrawn from traffic and stored at Doncaster Works. During 2002, 89001 was used at Bounds Green as a static ETH supply before being returned to Doncaster.

89001 entered preservation again with the AC Locomotive Group in December 2004 and returned to Barrow Hill, the group buying the loco from GNER in November 2006. The loco is now set for a return to the main line with Locomotive Services on railtour duties.

In the early years following electrification, Class 90s stood in for Class 91s on many occasions, working over the entire line before being restricted to the Leeds route during the GNER years. Class 90s also worked Edinburgh–North Berwick local services for ScotRail in 2004–05 due to an EMU shortage.

Class 90s were also hired in daily from Railfreight Distribution and EWS for use on Leeds services to compensate for low Class 91 availability. Reliability improvements and later refurbishment of the Class 91 fleet meant that the 90s were no longer required until brought in again from EWS's successor company, DB Schenker, in September 2016 by Virgin Trains for Leeds and Newark North Gate services, with occasional forays as far as Newcastle. The Class 90s were finally taken off hire with the introduction of the Azuma EMUs.

Following the announcement of the electrification of the ECML, the initial intention for BR was to introduce 140mph trains to replace the HSTs on most services. Costs and infrastructure issues prevented such running, but the tender was issued for high-speed capable stock. GEC won the tendering process for 31 locos, these to be built in two batches at Crewe Works (91001–10 and 91011–31) with a pause in production before the introduction of the second batch to iron out any issues found in operation. The first batch was produced between 1988 and 1989 and the second batch completed in 1991.

The design specifications for the Class 91s were demanding; the future-proof option for 140mph running, compatibility with other BR loco-hauled stock (it was envisaged they may be used on some sleeper trains

On 26 February 2017, 90039 waits at Leeds on a Virgin Trains East Coast service to King's Cross with the loco substituting for a Class 91.

90023 departs Peterborough, propelling a Leeds–King's Cross service south in September 1994.

and other services) and the option to haul future tilting stock at up to nine-degree cant deficiency, although this would have been principally for use on any WCML passenger duties. The Mk.4s also needed some design advances, as they were expected to run as smoothly at 140mph as the Mk.3s did at 125mph.

The Class 91s were the most powerful locos in the UK before the introduction of the Channel Tunnel shuttle stock, and initially they were used on Leeds services, deliveries beginning in early 1988. Initially, ten

91002 and 91007 stand at Newcastle on services from King's Cross on 10 May 1994. (Andy Flowers Collection)

91007 poses at Leeds on 5 August 1998 after arrival from London. Class 308 EMU 308165 stands alongside after arrival on a local service from Ilkley.

of the locos were put into traffic with a view to determining any modifications that may be needed to the remainder of the fleet. The initial modification programme proved successful, and Class 91s were allocated a number of King's Cross to Leeds diagrams from spring 1989, several months ahead of schedule. The Class 91s were delivered in the then standard InterCity livery with 91001, appropriately named *Swallow*.

91106 *East Lothian* at Newcastle on 8 February 2004 on the 08.30 Doncaster to Glasgow Central.

91027 approaches Doncaster on 27 March 1999 on a King's Cross to Edinburgh service. (Andy Flowers Collection)

With Mk.4 stock yet to be delivered, the only 125mph stock available for the new services with Class 91s were HST Mk.3 trailers. Unfortunately, HST stock operates on a specific three-phase AC electrical supply with conventional stock being powered by a single-phase supply from a locomotive. As a stopgap, a HST power car was used as a DVT and also to supply ETH to the eight-car HST rakes with the Class 91s used for traction. The power cars were fitted with buffers and drawgear for use on these duties to allow rescue by conventional locomotives or assistance in the event of any TDM issues.

After some issues with the HST power cars running in idle mode for extended periods, the decision was made to also use the diesel for tractive effort, the extra 2,250hp leading to some very lively performances.

Mk.4 stock was introduced on a King's Cross–Peterborough train in March 1989, and by May 1990, eight sets were in use on Leeds diagrams, and one from York. Around the same time, the Class 91s were popular on charter duties, making an interesting sight running blunt end first when travelling southbound and occasionally hauling air-braked Mk.1 stock.

On 26 September 1991, 91031 (now 91131) was used on a high-speed demonstration, achieving a three hour and 29 minutes non-stop run between London and Edinburgh. British regulations have since required in-cab signalling on any train running at speeds above 125mph, preventing the 140mph running on that day being legally attained in regular service.

BR later experimented with 140mph running by using a fifth flashing green aspect on the line between New England North and Stoke Tunnel, indicating the next signal is also green and allowing longer braking distances and higher speeds. The signalling is still in place, enabling test runs at speeds above 125mph.

91010 (now 91110) holds the speed record for a British locomotive, achieving 161.7mph on 17 September 1989 south of Little Bytham, on Stoke Bank, not far from where *Mallard* set the world steam speed record.

91030 arrives at Leeds in May 1997, on a service from King's Cross. After privatisation the previous year, the new operator of Great North Eastern Railways (GNER) was still in the process of rebranding the Class 91s and Mk.4 stock in its own colours, leading to the unusual use of mixed-liveried sets. (Andy Flowers Collection)

91028 arrives at Leeds on 15 February 1997 on a service from King's Cross. A Class 308 EMU waits in the background with a service for Ilkley.

A large-scale programme of reliability modifications carried out under GNER saw the fleet renumbered as 91101–22 and 91124–32. 91023 was renumbered, superstitiously, as 91132 following its involvement in the two fatal accidents at Great Heck and Hatfield.

When National Express East Coast (NXEC) took over the franchise, the GNER livery was initially modified with a white stripe applied over the red one before the full livery of diagonal broad bodyside silver-grey and white stripes was applied. When NXEC gave up the East Coast franchise in 2009, and Directly Operated Railways (branded as East Coast Trains) took over, the livery was changed to silver-grey with a narrow horizontal bodyside stripe.

The Class 91s were very intensively diagrammed, often working over 1,000 miles per day, including some services to Bradford, Skipton and Glasgow, with occasional diversions via Carlisle giving a chance to show their hill climbing abilities up Beattock. Even this late in their life, the class broke new ground from December 2019, working a service for LNER through to Stirling.

It was thought that as many as 20 of the Class 91 fleet might be exported to Eastern Europe for freight duties following their withdrawal from the ECML after Europhoenix bought 91117 and 91120 for regearing by Voit and trials. Plans envisaged the locos being semi-permanently coupled in pairs (with pointed cabs leading), although no orders were forthcoming.

Possibilities for further use for the Class 91s in the UK included open access operator Grand Union, which aimed to use the locos on Paddington to Cardiff and Euston to Stirling services from the end of 2020. Rail Operations Group also expressed an interest in buying several of the class for high-speed logistics services. Virgin Trains also proposed using Class 91s for an open-access service from Euston to Liverpool Lime Street. None of these plans came to fruition, and it is likely that most of the Class 91 fleet will be withdrawn after they finish their LNER duties in a few years' time.

Electric Locomotives

On 6 February 2020, 'celebrity' InterCity Class 91 91119 *Bounds Green* pauses at York on a service from King's Cross to Edinburgh Waverley.

91119 stands at King's Cross on 9 October 2021 on 1N32, the 19.30 departure to York.

91125 stands at King's Cross on 11 August 2002 with a Leeds service. Operating blunt end first restricted the speed to 110mph, but this was not so much of an issue on the Leeds trains, where similarly restricted Class 90s were also used.

On 7 July 2001, 91112 *County of Cambridgeshire* propels its King's Cross-bound train away from Grantham.

Chapter 17

Azumas

The replacement of the Class 91 fleet has been a long, protracted process with tenders for the Azuma units (or IETs) being issued as far back as 2007 by the Department for Transport (DfT). At the time, trials of the new stock were due to begin in 2012 with HSTs to be replaced first from March 2015. As it turned out, the Great Western IETs entered service first in October 2017.

Agility Trains is the consortium formed to deliver the IET programme, consisting of Hitachi (rolling stock manufacturer) and John Laing with AXA (investment). Agility was announced as the preferred bidder in February 2009. Following a delay due to a change of government, a review of costs and changes to the Great Western Main Line electrification scheme, the final deal between the DfT and Agility for a 27½-year supply and maintenance contract was signed in July 2012.

Azuma running on electric power on the northern section of the ECML was delayed by two main issues, the level of power available in the overheads and electro-magnetic current problems, leading to signalling interference. Before the introduction of the Azumas, around one third of East Coast services

On 7 November 2019, Azuma 800111 prepares to leave for Newcastle.

On 7 November 2019, 91115 prepares for departure from York on a King's Cross to Edinburgh service.

Driving Van Trailer (DVT) 82213 passes through Newark North Gate on 5 May 2022 on 1D07, the 09.03 King's Cross to Leeds, hauled by 91107.

were provided by HSTs. With the changeover to an all-electric fleet on the electrified East Coast, further infrastructure was needed including, initially, a new feeder station at Potteric Carr, just south of Doncaster. The final members of the 65 strong Azuma fleet entered traffic in 2020, and the remaining Class 91s will be withdrawn from service in a few years' time.

Chapter 18

Nationalisation to Privatisation

From nationalisation on 1 January 1948, the line became part of British Railways and the timetable was accelerated with diesels introduced from the late 1950s and upgrades of certain sections to 100mph running in the 1960s. The first length of 100mph line was completed on 15 June 1965, a 17-mile stretch between Peterborough and Grantham. Upgrades continued in the 1970s with the introduction of 125mph running with HSTs. Electrification, completed in 1991, enabled further acceleration of services following the introduction of Class 91s and Mk.4 stock.

The year 1996 saw privatisation and a period of major organisational changes on the line. In April 1996, Sea Containers was given a seven-year franchise to operate the former InterCity East Coast division of BR under the marketing brand Great North Eastern Railways. The new operator adopted a 'midnight blue' livery (in use on the continental trains of sister company VSOE) with gold GNER lettering applied to the lower bodysides on HST power cars and Class 91s and a broad red waist band. Services began on 28 April 1996, with the TOC being one of the more successful of the private operators emerging from privatisation.

91130 *City of Newcastle* **waits at King's Cross on 23 October 2007, very unusually dragging a HST on a service to Newcastle.**

On 25 February 2022, 91119 *Bounds Green* pauses at Doncaster on 1D21, the 16.03 King's Cross to Leeds service. 91119 had been re-liveried into heritage InterCity colours by LNER in 2019 to commemorate 30 years in service and the impending withdrawal of the fleet.

GNER was later given a two-year extension to the franchise by the Strategic Rail Authority to operate trains until April 2005 in return for a programme of improvements, including rolling stock refurbishment and additional coaches.

In addition to the refurbishment of the Mk.4 fleet, spare Class 373 Eurostar sets were hired in for extra services, and HSTs were lengthened by one coach. The Eurostars operated from King's Cross to York from 2000 to 2002 and were transferred on to the more lucrative Leeds route from 2002 until the end of the lease arrangement in December 2005. GNER went on to win a renewal of the franchise up to 2015, although the award included a commitment to pay an annual sum of £130m to the government, putting a strain on finances.

On 17 October 2019, 43317, with 43315 at the rear, waits at Edinburgh Waverley after arrival on a service from King's Cross. HSTs are still seen at Edinburgh on CrossCountry services and internal ScotRail trains to Aberdeen and Inverness.

91127 passes Eaton (a foot crossing south of Retford) on 24 November 2011 on a service for King's Cross from Newcastle. (Andy Flowers Collection)

Eurostar power car 3312 arrives at Peterborough on a service from Leeds to King's Cross in June 2004. Power car 3311 brought up the rear.

91128 pauses at Grantham on 22 September 2015 on a Leeds to King's Cross service.

Soaring passenger numbers meant even more capacity was needed, and GNER planned to buy withdrawn Mk.3 sleeping coaches for conversion to open passenger stock, although technical and financial issues saw this plan abandoned.

Sea Containers filed for bankruptcy in October 2006, and on 15 December 2006, the DfT announced it would invite new bids for the ECML franchise with GNER allowed to run the franchise as a management contract until a new operator was found. On 15 January 2007, bids were submitted to the DfT for the new InterCity East Coast franchise but GNER did not make the shortlist.

The DfT announced on 14 August 2007 that NXEC Trains Ltd, part of the National Express Group, had won the franchise, which would be branded as National Express East Coast and due to run from 9 December 2007 to 31 March 2015.

On 26 April 2018, 91126 propels a Newcastle-King's Cross train south out of Durham.

After NXEC also ran into financial difficulties, the East Coast franchise was formed by the DfT, which took the train operating company back into public ownership between 14 November 2009 and 28 February 2015. After retendering, the franchise was awarded to Virgin Trains East Coast on 1 March 2015, with a view to operating it until 2023. After more financial difficulties, the franchise was ended early and since June 2018 has once again been operated under DfT control, with the new franchise reviving the older LNER name.

91127 *Edinburgh Castle* **leaves York on a King's Cross to Edinburgh service on 6 March 2007.**

Chapter 19

Performance

The ECML is renowned as a high-speed running track and has long been used as a test bed for record breaking and testing, including the exploits of *Mallard*, HSTs, the APT and more recently the Class 91s.

Even the departure from King's Cross, weaving through the congested inner suburban running lines, is relatively quick. After the departure from King's Cross and the testing 1 in 107 climb through Gas Works and Copenhagen Tunnels, by 12½ miles out, at the summit of the eight-mile long 1 in 200 climb to Potters Bar, trains are/were typically running at the following speeds (loco-hauled trains all having a trailing load of eight coaches):

- Class 31: 58mph.
- Class 47: 80mph.
- Class 312: 87mph.
- Class 55: 92mph.
- HST: 105mph.

On 5 May 2022, Azuma unit 801203 arrives at Newark North Gate on 1E04, the 06.56 Edinburgh Waverley to London King's Cross. The new units, while lacking the glamour of many of their streamlined predecessors, are setting new speed records on the ECML.

Chapter 20
The Future

At the time of writing, some issues with the Azuma fleet have meant that some Class 91s were being given a stay of execution for slightly longer than originally planned. Even with this unplanned delay, the Class 91 fleet is still not expected to last in service on the East Coast after 2023/24, and readers are recommended to enjoy the locos and Mk.4 coaches while they can.

On 14 September 2019, 91128 waits at Doncaster on a Kings' Cross to Leeds service.

91111 *For the Fallen* stands at King's Cross on 9 October 2021 with 1D30, the 19.33 to Bradford Forster Square. 91111 has been re-liveried and carries crests in dedication to the army regiments along the east coast route.

Other books you might like:

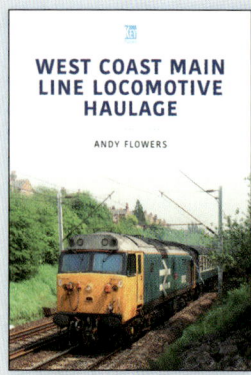
Britain's Railways Series, Vol. 24

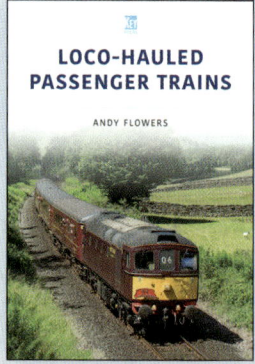
Britain's Railways Series, Vol. 1

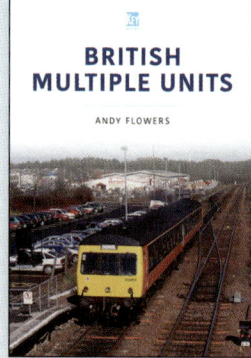
Britain's Railways Series, Vol. 13

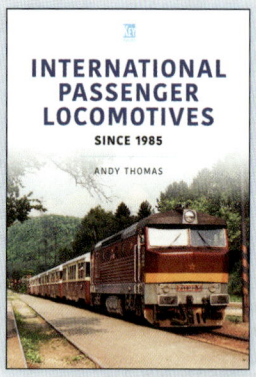
World Railways Series, Vol. 1

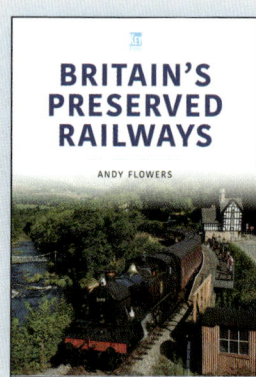
Britain's Railways Series, Vol. 1

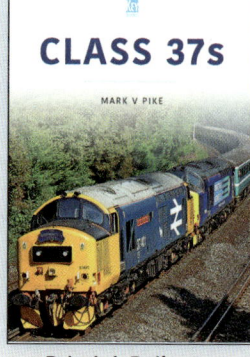
Britain's Railways Series, Vol. 23

For our full range of titles please visit:
shop.keypublishing.com/books

VIP Book Club

Sign up today and receive
TWO FREE E-BOOKS

Be the first to find out about our forthcoming book releases and receive exclusive offers.

Register now at **keypublishing.com/vip-book-club**

Our VIP Book Club is a 100% spam-free zone, and we will never share your email with anyone else. You can read our full privacy policy at: privacy.keypublishing.com